Country & Western LINE DANCING

Step-by-Step Instructions for Cowgirls & Cowboys

Judy Dygdon & Tony Conger

Illustrations by Tony Conger

Published by
Sigma Press, 1 South Oak Lane, Wilmslow, Cheshire, SK9 6AR, England.

British Library Cataloguing in Publication Data
A CIP record for this book is available from the British Library.

ISBN: 1-85058-583-0

Typsetting and Design by: Sigma Press, Wilmslow, Cheshire.

Cover Design: The Agency, Wilmslow

Printed by: MFP Design & Print

Before you begin

Words, words, words . . .

Line Dancing began in the USA and has become popular elsewhere, including the UK! We are delighted that Judy & Tony, authors of this book, are both American. They live in Crete, Illinois and they are both members of the National Teachers Association for Country & Western Dance. The music on the CD is performed by a group from New Jersey, so everything is as American as Apple Pie!

In order to preserve the authenticity of Line Dancing, we have deliberately retained American spellings such as "color", but a few terms may be unfamiliar to British readers: a "trunk" on a car is a "boot", an "elevator" is a "lift"; "counter-clockwise" is the same as "anti-clockwise" and so on. Oh yes, and your "tush" is your backside!

None of this is likely to cause confusion, but there is one opportunity to soak up some American culture: the "shuffle pattern" for "Reggae Cowboy II" uses baseball terminology. UK readers who have been on the planet Zog for their entire lives should note that baseball is a little like rounders!

But I can't find . . .

There are, literally, thousands of Line Dances so this book really is just the tip of the iceberg. The dances described include many of the most popular ones, but you may hear them called by other names. Here are some that we know about:

Dance Name	***Also Known As***
Bartender's Stomp	Electric Horseman
Bayou Bangle	Reggae Cowboy II
Black Velvet	Ski Bumpus
Charleston Cha Cha	Cowboy Charleston
Charleston Rock	Cowboy Boogie
Charleston Tap	Cowboy Charleston
Crazy Feet	Applejack
Ming Boogie	Cowboy Boogie
Southside Shuffle	Swingin' Gate
Watergate	Cowboy Boogie
White Horse	Ski Bumpus

About the Music

In this book, there are over 50 dances but, on the CD, there are just 12 tracks. These have been *very* carefully selected so that each track can be used for several dances. Naturally, we would like you to know about the people who first sang them, so that you can, if you wish, obtain full-length albums by the original artists. The copyright information is all listed on the copyright page of this book, and here is a list of the original recording artists:

Song	**Originally Recorded By**
Walkin' Away A Winner	Kathy Mattea
The City Put The Country Back In Me	Neil McCoy
Talk Some	Billy Ray Cyrus
I Wanna Go Too Far	Trisha Yearwood
Fast As You	Dwight Yoakam
The South's Gonna Do It Again	The Charlie Daniels Band
I'm So Miserable Without You	Billy Ray Cyrus
Shut Up And Kiss Me	Mary Chapin Carpenter
Wher'm I Gonna Live When I Get Home	Billy Ray Cyrus
(You Got Me Over) a Heartache Tonight	Dolly Parton
Redneck Girl	The Bellamy Brothers
Gulf of Mexico	Clint Black

Our versions of the songs were recorded by 'The Rustlers' at Sound & Fury Productions and Mast Audio, NY/NJ. We thank Rusty Cutchin of Sound & Fury for doing such an excellent job and for sticking to a tight schedule!

Contents

Level II

Level III

Level IV

Dances A-Z

Getting Started

Some Observations on the Development of a Country and Western Dancer

It was the autumn of 1986. We had been invited to a party at a nightclub. Music and dancing, we knew, would be a big part of the evening and we really had not done this before. Nevertheless, Judy was surprised when I said to her, "Now, before we go in, I just want you to know, *I don't dance*."

Judy was mildly disappointed, but looked forward to being with friends and listening to music. Throughout the evening we did just that: talked with friends, listened to recorded popular music from the 50s, 60s and 70s, and watched people dance. The dancing we watched was mostly the freestyle dance that accompanied rock and roll music. Judy did not mention that she would like to dance, taking me at my "I don't dance" words. So she was shocked when, late in the evening, I turned to her and said, "Come on, let's dance." Level one had been attained: we liked to dance.

After that evening, we occasionally looked for opportunities to dance, and had fun. In the spring of 1990, work took me to Houma, Louisiana for several days. Houma (pronounced "home-ah"), mentioned in several Country and Western songs, is a small town in the bayou country, south-east of New Orleans. It is a great place for tours of the swamps (especially Miss Annie's) and for eating crawfish and boudin sausage. Judy visited one weekend. On a Saturday evening, after dinner with my co-workers, we looked for a place to go to continue our visit, listen to music, and maybe do a little of the freestyle dancing that had now become a favorite pastime. We ended up at "The Country Club" which we assumed was a country *club* (in the U.S., a golf/tennis club with a restaurant or bar for social gathering). It had all the requisite elements: music, a bar, and a dance floor. As usual, we listened, we drank some beer (Lone Star "longnecks"), and we danced to some rock and roll music. Although a lot of people were wearing cowboy hats and boots, this just appeared to be a local custom. Little did we know that we had entered a *country* club. We learned that quickly, however. A Country and Western song began and, as we watched in amazement, the dance floor filled with people in regimented lines, and they were all doing exactly the same thing! We looked at each other and instantly knew that we had to learn more about this. Level two had been attained: we wanted to line dance.

We had, we thought, picked up the fundamentals of two-stepping, and we tried this at Nashville North, a Country and Western bar near Chicago's O'Hare Airport. Friendly dancers there tried to help us (we have met many friendly, helpful Country and Western dancers!), but it took us a little while to find a way to learn more about line dancing. In fact, it took moving from Chicago to Crete, Illinois. The village of Crete (population 6,100) is located south of Chicago, where city meets country.

During our first summer in Crete, we attended a "street dance". At this dance, we once again found ourselves among line dancers and we stumbled through our first lesson of the "Duchess Hustle". But we wanted to learn all those other dances we had seen people do. This led us to enrol in our first C&W line dance class. Level three had been attained: we learned some dances.

We owe a great deal to the people who taught us our first steps, Cheryl Scott and Norman Schnepf (friends and instructors), and to the other people from whom we subsequently took lessons, especially the Lovin' Country Dance Club (at Rockin' Ranch in Crown Point, Indiana), and Bob and Faith Brown of the Amarillo Star Dance Club. We also thank the instructors and helpful dancers at the various *country* clubs throughout northern Illinois and Indiana. Yet, for all the lessons we had, we had to get out there on the floor and dance. That was a big step, but when we took it we found that we could make mistakes and still enjoy ourselves.

We trust that the fact that you are reading this book means that you have the passed the first two levels of becoming a Country and Western line dancer:

1. You want to dance

2. You want to line dance

That leaves only three more levels:

3. Learning some steps

4. Having the courage to get up and dance

5. Having the humility to persist even when your feet and brain don't want to cooperate.

Steps 4 and 5 are easier to achieve when you practice, practice, practice. (A longneck or two might help for level 4, but it sure brings about the need for humility at level 5.)

Welcome to Line Dancin'

The dances we have selected for this book represent a variety of types and difficulty levels. Some of the dances are old and some are new, but all of them are currently being taught or danced in our region. The dance steps and terminology reflect our region's dance styles: in other parts of the U.S., you may well find the same basic dances being done, with subtle variations in certain steps. This "regionalism" is part of the fun of Country and Western dancing. When we travel through the U.S., we often find people doing a dance that looks familiar, but with some different steps. Once you know a form of a dance, it is not too difficult to identify that dance when it is done in a different regional style. (Actually, it is not too different from trying to understand what someone is saying when you are both speaking the same language but with different regional dialects or accents.)

Enjoy learning the dances in this book. And remember, there will always be new dances to learn, techniques to master, and embellishments to perfect.

A Brief History of Country and Western Dancing

These days, as Country and Western dancing is gaining popularity across the world, it is not uncommon to hear people ask where it originated. We are surprised to find that some people assume Country and Western dancing *started* with the release of an early 1980s movie, *Urban Cowboy*, or that it was a brainstorm of dancers who had tired of "disco". Neither frequently made assumption is warranted, as Country and Western dancing has been around, as a folk-dancing form, for some considerable time.

Most cultures have some form of folk, or social, non-professional dance in their histories (e.g. English round and square dances which date back to Medieval times, German schottisches, Spanish fandangoes and African juba dancing). Dance historians tell us that folk-dancing blossoms in areas that are isolated from professional dance. Given the geographic distances involved, and the speed with which information travelled, it is difficult to imagine an area more isolated than the American West in the middle 1800s. It seems conditions were right for the development of a new folk-dancing style, and the beginnings of Country and Western dancing, as we know it today, were formed.

The look of Country and Western dancing reminds many of other, older, folk-dance forms. This, too, is not surprising when one considers the population of the American West during this time. People from a wide variety of cultures (European – especially English, German, Irish, French and Spanish; North American – Mexican and native American; and African), each with different folk-dance histories, went into this mix. Country and western dancing, which looks a little bit like many other folk-dance styles, but not exactly like any, is what emerged.

In its early days, and continuing today, the Country and Western dance tradition is made up of four forms:

- The line dances (drill, spoke, and contra), in which people dance singly, mostly in one place on the dance floor, executing identical, planned moves;

- round dances, in which people dance around the floor with partners, executing identical, planned moves;
- square dances, in which people dance in formations of 4 couples, executing identical moves chosen by a "caller";
- and the partnered freestyle dances of two step, polka, waltz and later, Cha Cha and swing.

Country and Western dancing is certainly enjoying a revival of interest these days. Many of the dances being done are old; more are very new. Line and round dances are being choreographed by dancers in the United States and in several other countries. Country and western dancing has certainly achieved trend status. The reasons for the trend are not entirely clear. Perhaps Country and Western dancing appeals to many because of the music to which it is danced. Perhaps it is popular because Country and Western dancing has now become more professional: you can take lessons in it and there are competitions for dancers and choreographers (you can even read books about it!). Many people enjoy Country and Western dancing because you can dance even if you don't have a partner. Whatever the reasons for the trend, Country and Western dancing was not born with the trend, and it will not die when the trend has run its course.

If you would like to learn more about the history of Country and Western dancing, we suggest you consult the following books:

Dance Across Texas by Betty Casey (University of Texas Press, 1985)

Kicker Dancin' Texas Style by Shirley Rushing and Patrick McMillan (Hunter Textbooks, 1988)

Before you Start to Dance

What you Need to Know about Music

Dances are choreographed to match the rhythm, or beats, in a piece of music. Before you try to learn dances, you must be able to hear the rhythm in music. You probably are already able to do that, but, if you are not, spending some time listening to music and trying to tap out its rhythm will be time well invested in your dancing future. Our dance descriptions are written in terms of the beats of music which a set of steps should match. It is the beats which signal you to move.

Some hints: the rhythm is usually expressed by a percussion instrument – a drum, for example. You will be able to detect repeating patterns of four evenly spaced beats (4/4 time, or variants of it), and repeating patterns of three evenly spaced beats (3/4 or waltz time). There are also patterns in which half beats are pronounced, as in country Cha Cha rhythms. In contrast to the *one*, *two*, *three*, *four*, of 4/4 time, in Cha Cha patterns, you should be able to hear a percussion instrument on beats *one*, *two*, *three*, *and*, *four*.

Any dance can be done to many pieces of music of similar rhythm. In addition to rhythm, music varies in tempo, or speed (often described in "beats per minute" or "bpm"). As it is easier to learn a dance doing it slowly, but more challenging to do a dance you know well, quickly, we suggest music for practicing and music for dancing. (When you first try a dance to faster music, you may find it easier if you take smaller steps.) Our dancing music suggestions identify songs with which that dance works well, or for which it is particularly popular. Do not feel limited by our suggestions. Pay attention to the rhythm of each dance and enjoy trying it to other songs.

We have organized our presentation of line dances into groups of dances done to basic 4/4 time, country Cha Cha, and waltz rhythms. Oddly, not all line dances are done in a line. For this reason, this book includes two sections of non-line, line dances: dances done in a circle and dances done with pairs of lines facing each other, or "contra" style.

What you Need to Know about Country and Western Dance Floor Etiquette

In Country and Western dance halls, line dancing, in which people typically dance singly and do not travel across much of the floor, is often accompanied by stationary or "slot" couples' dances (like swing) and couples' dances (pattern, two-step, and polka) which move around the floor. In order to allow room for all three of these forms of country dancing, a few simple rules must be followed. Line dancing, unless otherwise dictated by house rules, is done in the center of the dance floor, allowing room for travelling couples' dances on the outside perimeter and "slot" couples' dances just inside the ring of dancers travelling the perimeter.

When you do line dancing, it is important to remember that part of the beauty of these dances is the regularity of the lines. When you join a dance on the floor, make sure you are: facing the same direction as the other dancers, positioned squarely behind the person in front of you, and in a straight line with the people next to you. Often two or more different line dances will take place in the center of a dance floor. When this happens, each group must allow room for the pattern of the others.

If you are at a club with a disc jockey, the D.J. may make suggestions for a dance to accompany the next song. If you know that dance, join in. Dances typically begin facing the bandstand, and with the onset of lyrics. It pays to know your dance music, as your feet must be ready to move at the same time that the lyrics begin. Sometimes, someone very familiar with the song will "cue" the others on when to begin a dance, often by counting down *"six, seven, eight"*. When you do any of the dances in this book, assume that the pattern should begin with the lyrics. We alert you to the rare dances for which this is not the case in the "About this Dance" section of the dance descriptions.

What you Need to Know about Country and Western Dance Style

In traditional Country and Western dancing, foot movements (with the attached legs) are primary. Hip movements (rocks, bumps) and hand claps or boot slaps also come into play. Generally, the arms and hands (except when needed for a clap or slap) should be placed out of the way. A woman can hold her hands behind her back, or one or both hands can be placed on the belt in front. Women are allowed some stylistic leeway in the use of arms and hands, but C&W dancin' ain't no ballet! A man should put his hands on his belt or hook the thumbs in the belt or front pockets. This will help maintain that slightly detached air. "Cowboys" do not flail or dangle their arms – even when doing spins or turns. When you do not use your arms for momentum, spins and turns are much more challenging to do. This adds some legitimacy to those claims of the athletic skill required by Country and Western dancing!

Arm Position

A la seconde A la belt

"... Line Dancin' ain't no ballet! ..."

What you Need to Know about your Feet

The dance descriptions in this book will tell you *where* and *how* to place *what* part of your foot. Please read the following before attempting to follow the dance descriptions.

What: *Foot Parts*

In the dance descriptions, you will sometimes see us refer to the toe, heel and ball of the foot. When "toe", "heel", or "ball" is mentioned in the step line, it is important for styling that you execute the move using the part mentioned. When an instruction is given for "foot", you may do the movement as it is most comfortable for you.

How: *Foot Orientations*

Parallel Indicates that one foot is held in essentially the same direction as the other foot. "Parallel" for you should be your comfortable standing position.

Turned out Indicates that the toe of one foot points diagonally away from the other. When the right foot is "turned out", its toe points diagonally right. When the left foot is "turned out", its toe points diagonally left.

Positions of Right Foot

Turned in Indicates that the toe of one foot points diagonally toward the other foot. When the right foot is "turned in", its toe points diagonally left. When the left foot is "turned in", its toe points diagonally right.

When it is important for styling, we use "parallel", "turned out", and "turned in" to tell you how to hold your foot when making a particular move. We do not often tell you how to hold your foot. If no particular instruction is given, assume that the parallel orientation works best.

Where: *Foot Locations*

Home: describes a position in which your feet are directly under your body and are parallel to one another. For example, when you are instructed to move your right foot "home", you are to return it to a comfortable standing position under your right hip.

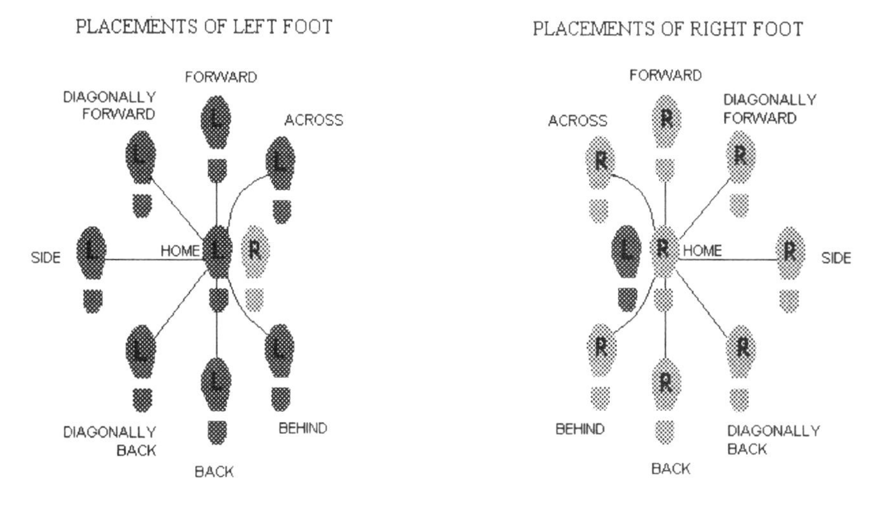

Locations for foot placements

("Home" is sometimes used to refer to your starting position on the dance floor, but that definition will not be used in this book.)

Place: Sometimes you will be told to execute a foot action without changing the foot's location. In these cases, you will be told to do the action "in place". For example, if you are told to "step right foot in place", you are to put weight on your right foot, wherever it was after your preceding move.

Several other locations need to be defined before we can begin. We find that these other locations are best defined by the "Locations for foot placements" diagram. This diagram provides you with the names of the locations to which your feet will be directed in step descriptions.

What you Need to Know about this Book's Organization

Country and western line dances are sequences of steps that form a pattern. Line dancing is done by repeating the pattern for the duration of a piece of music. The patterns range from those that consist of only a few, relatively simple steps, to very lengthy arrangements of intricate moves. As in anything else, if you are just beginning to learn line dancing, you will be more successful if you begin with the easier dances and move to the more difficult. For this reason, we have organized the dance descriptions in this book according to their complexity. Within each category, the dances that appear early are generally made up of fewer and less complicated steps, or are designed to be done more slowly, than the dances that appear later. We have assigned a difficulty rating (from I to IV) to each of the dances in this book to communicate our judgement of its difficulty. The dances are presented, within each dance category, in ascending order of difficulty.

If you are new to dancing, we recommend that you try to learn the dances in the order in which they appear as mastering the earlier dances will help you to learn the later dances. Preceding the step by step description for each dance is detailed instruction in how to do the steps and combinations that are used for the first time in that particular dance.

If you are not new to dancing, you may wish to learn these dances as they appeal to you. If you try to learn these dances in a different order from the sequence we have used, please remember to check the Glossary for detailed instruction on any step or combination that is new to you.

Many of the steps, or individual foot movements, that make up dances are used so frequently and in so many dances that they have special names. Individual steps can also often be grouped into *combinations*, or sequences of steps that frequently recur and are used in a variety of dances. In other words, individual *steps* are put together in *combinations*. *Combinations* are put together in different ways to form *dances*. If you can learn to see dances, not as sequences of many steps, but as patterns of a few combinations, you will find dances easier to learn, and easier to remember. Ultimately, this ability should make it easier for you to learn new dances simply by watching someone do them.

Understanding the Dance Pages

New Concepts, Steps and Combinations

We open our presentation of each dance with detailed descriptions of the new steps, combinations, and other dance concepts found in that dance. The terms we use to identify individual foot movements and combinations are consistent with those recommended by the National Teachers' Association for Country and Western Dance (NTA) and the British Western Dance Association (BWDA). Some terms used by Country and Western dance choreographers and teachers are not yet part of NTA's vocabulary: we have also included those terms. If you are learning the dances in order, you will be instructed in steps and combinations as you need them. If you prefer to learn dances in an order different from the one we have chosen, remember that you can always refer to the Glossary for detailed information on steps, combinations and dance concepts.

The Dance

Of course, most of the dance pages are devoted to the choreography: the step by step descriptions. However, other useful information is also provided. Before the step descriptions, we provide some basic information about the dance: difficulty level, choreographer, number of directions the dance faces, and the number of beats in the dance pattern. You will also find suggested music for practicing and dancing. In particular, note the references to the ***Free CD*** which accompanies this book. After the step descriptions, we have included three other tools we believe will be useful to you:

The Variations: Part of the fun of line dancing for many people is the challenge of mastering the specific steps and combinations. If you are one of these people, we attempt to add to your challenge and to your fun. Following several dance descriptions, we suggest "variations" for you to try after you have mastered the basic dance. A variation might be a new way to do a combination, perhaps by adding a turn, or a replacement set of more difficult steps. It isn't necessary for you to try the variations, but they are there for you to explore.

The Rhythm Line: The "rhythm line" summarizes the dancer's foot and hand movements with the rhythm and tempo of the music. Dance music tempo can roughly be categorized as slow, medium or fast. In preparing rhythm lines, we have chosen 90, 120 and 180 beats per minute to represent slow, medium and fast tempos, respectively. For each dance, we display the beats and movements under a timeline which represents the tempo to which the dance is most often done.

The Cues: We also include a tool we call "cues". In this section we offer a "cue" or reminder for every step of the dance. Most often, these are simple, one syllable words. While you cannot learn a dance from the cues alone, once you have reviewed the steps of a dance, saying the cues to yourself as you practice should help you remember the steps. The cues can also be useful for a dance instructor to call aloud as a class practices a new dance.

Step Descriptions

We should like to explain a little about the format we have chosen for the presentation of each dance's steps. Under the heading "BEAT – DESCRIPTION" you will see levels of information that look something like the following:

Beat	Description	
	Boot Hook and Swivels	<— Section Line
1-4	Left boot hook combination	<— Combination Line
	1 Touch **left** heel forward	<— Step Line
	2 Hook **left** foot in front of **right** leg	<— Step Line
	3 Touch **left** heel forward	<— Step Line
	4 Step **left** foot next to **right** foot	<— Step Line
5	Swivel heels to left	<— Step Line
6	Swivel heels to center	<— Step Line

The Section Lines: We have included SECTION labels to help you remember portions of the dance. Many dances can be easily divided into sections of similar movements. The SECTION labels will not tell you what to do in detail, but they will help you remember the kinds of movements that are coming next in the dance.

The Combination Lines: In contrast to SECTION, "Combination Name" will tell you what to do and, once you have some experience in dancing, the combination name is probably all you will need to look at in order to execute the appropriate sequence of movements. You can tell when you are looking at a combination name because it is always preceded by a range of beats (for example, 1-4, as above; 1-&; 1-2; etc.). Combinations always consist of more than one movement so they always are associated with more than one point in time.

The Step Lines: If you are new to dancing, or if you encounter a combination name that is new to you, you will need to check the third level of information provided. This information is inset under the combination name and gives you step by step information on how to do a particular sequence of movements.

Dances also include a variety of specific steps that are not included in combinations. In these cases, the step lines appear as lines 5 and 6 appear in the sample above. Note that these lines are not inset.

In a step line, we adhere to a strict format for describing foot movements: action, foot, location. The first term you see will tell you what kind of movement or action is to be done. The second term tells you what foot is to do the movement. The third expression tells you the location in which the foot will be placed.

In the individual step instructions, we always boldface "right", "left", and "both" when they are used to identify feet so that you quickly can determine which foot is to move. We have tried to minimize confusion between feet and directions of movements by showing the foot in bold face (for example, "**left** foot") but showing directions in regular font (for example, "turn left").

Most of the time, only one foot action is required for each beat of the dance pattern. Sometimes, two foot movements are required for a single beat of music. When this is the case, we connect the two instructions with "and". When you see this, know that you are to execute both movements simultaneously. To minimize confusion, we have adopted the following rule for beats involving two movements: we describe the first movement in our "Action, Foot, Location" format. If the second movement is done with the same foot as the first, the second movement is described by "Action, Location". If the second movement is done with a different foot than the first movement, it is described by "Action, Foot, Location".

When a body or hand motion, as opposed to a foot motion, is required for a particular beat of music, we put the direction at the end of the step line.

By the way, don't be alarmed if the terms used in the sample ("boot hook, touch, swivel" etc.) don't make sense to you now. In this book, you will be given clear instructions on how to make every movement as it is needed for a dance.

ARE YOU SURE THIS IS HOW TO PRACTICE "TENNESSEE TWISTER"?

Dances done to 4/4 time rhythms in drill lines

Introduction to the Dances

The dances in this section are done to music played in 4/4 time (or other even rhythm). Besides rhythm, these dances have in common the fact that they are danced in drill lines. This means that each dancer positions him/herself on the dance floor so that the dancer is directly behind one dancer and directly alongside another. Viewed from above, the dance floor should look like a perfect grid.

In taking your position on the dance floor for a drill line dance, look for a vacancy in the "grid", being sure to have space around you so that you are able to execute the moves of the dance without crowding anyone else. Remember also that, on many Country and Western dance floors, some dancers may choose to do partner pattern or freestyle dances instead of the line dance. These dancers use the outside of the dance floor and circle around it as they dance. When you choose your position in a line dance, be sure to leave that outside circle clear.

Since much of the music you will hear when you dance these dances has four beats per measure, we have chosen to present steps in clusters of four. We believe this helps the dancer organize and remember the movements in a dance. Sometimes we deviate from this "cluster of four" rule. When we do that it is because we believe that, for a particular dance, an alternative organization will be better for helping you remember the steps.

The dances in the section will fit with any music in 4/4 rhythm (or variants of 4/4 rhythm). However, 4/4 rhythm music varies in tempo (the speed with which the music is played) and the mood of the melody. In each dance description we make suggestions for songs you might enjoy for that dance. We also present the rhythm line for the tempo to which the dance is most typically done.

Level I

The Freeze

About this dance: The Freeze is an established country dance. The version of the dance which follows is the one that is currently danced in our area. An earlier Freeze was very much like the Electric Slide: it differed only in that it moved in opposite directions! Apparently, The Freeze got its name from the manner in which that earlier Freeze was danced. Occasionally, someone would shout "freeze, 2, 3, 4" and all dancers would stand motionless on counts 13, 14, 15, and 16. This "freezing" is more readily done in the Electric Slide than in today's Freeze.

New Concepts, Steps and Combinations

New Concepts

Turn Indicates that the orientation of your body (direction or wall that you face) will change. There are different kinds of turns (pivot, military turn, etc.) and each will be defined as needed. Instructions to turn will specify a direction and amount of turn. Sometimes, dancers become confused with the direction specified for a turn. To turn left means to turn counter-clockwise. One way to ensure that you are turning in the prescribed direction is to think of your shoulders. In a turn to the *left*, you will turn toward your left shoulder. Your *left shoulder will move backwards*, while your right shoulder moves forward. Similarly, in a turn to the *right*, you will turn toward your right shoulder. Your *right shoulder will move backwards*, while your left shoulder moves forward. The amount of turn may be given as fractions of a full circle (1/8, 1/4, 1/2, etc.) or in degrees (90 degrees, 180 degrees, etc.)

New Steps

Hitch Instructs you to bend your knee and raise your leg. During a hitch, the thigh of the hitching leg should be almost parallel to the floor. The feet should be parallel to each other. (Some cowgirls and cowboys rightly believe that if they can hitch their thigh parallel to the floor, their jeans are too big!)

Pivot Instructs you to turn. The amount of the turn will be specified (1/4 or 90 degrees, 1/2 or 180 degrees, etc.), as will the direction of the turn (right or left). Pivots are usually done on the ball of the designated foot (or feet), however, on occasion a pivot is done on the heel of one foot and the ball of the other. Pivots are easier if you "prepare" your pivoting foot by slightly pointing it in the direction of the turn before you step down to pivot.

For example, "pivot on **left** foot ¼ turn left" instructs you to turn 90 degrees left while your weight is supported by your left foot. You would begin this move by pointing your left foot diagonally left. The move is completed by pivoting the rest of the ¼ turn on the ball of your left foot.

Slide

Instructs you to move the designated foot while keeping it lightly in contact with the floor. This move produces a look of the foot being pulled from one position to the next. When a slide is completed, all or most of the weight is on the sliding foot. Note that a slide is different from a slide-up. In a slide, the sliding foot bears weight; in a slide-up, it does not.

For example, "slide **right** foot next to **left** foot" instructs you to move your right foot from its last position to a position next to your left foot, keeping your right foot lightly in contact with the floor. As you finish the move, put all or most of your weight on the right foot.

Step

Instructs you to position your foot at the identified location and to transfer all or most of your weight to that foot. The amount of weight transferred usually depends on the sequence of steps.
For example, "step **right** foot forward" instructs you to position your right foot ahead of your left (as though you were walking forward), with your weight supported on your right foot, leaving your left foot ready to move next.

New Combinations

Vine

Instructs you to make a three step sideways movement to three beats of music. A vine will be described as either a right vine or left vine, indicating the direction of movement and the foot that moves first. On the first beat, the designated foot will move to the side. On the second beat, the other foot is crossed behind the first before it steps down. On the third beat, the foot that was first to move, moves again to the side.

For example, "right vine" instructs you to: step your right foot to the right, step your left foot behind your right, step your right foot to the right.

When vines are used in 4/4 time music, a fourth, "finishing move" for the foot that is free to move after the vine is often specified with the vine. For example, you will see directions such as "right vine with left scuff" or "left vine with right touch".

The Dance

Difficulty Level: I

Choreographer: Unknown

Dance Faces: four directions

Pattern Length: 16 Beats

Suggested Music:

For practicing – "I'm So Miserable Without You" – originally recorded by Billy Ray Cyrus (Track 7 on your ***Free CD***).

For dancing – "I'm So Miserable Without You" – originally recorded by Billy Ray Cyrus (Track 7 on your ***Free CD***). "Elvira" by Oak Ridge Boys

---

Beats	Description
	Vines
1-4	Right vine with left hitch
	1 Step **right** foot to right side
	2 Step **left** foot behind **right** foot
	3 Step **right** foot to right side
	4 Hitch **left** leg
5-8	Left vine with right hitch
	5 Step **left** foot to left side
	6 Step **right** foot behind **left** foot
	7 Step **left** foot to left side
	8 Hitch **right** leg
	Walk Back
9	Step **right** foot back
10	Step **left** foot back
11	Step **right** foot back
12	Hitch **left** leg
	Forward and Turn
13	Step **left** foot forward
14	Slide **right** foot next to **left** foot
15	Step **left** foot forward
16	Hitch **right** leg and pivot on **left** foot 1/4 turn left

Repeat Pattern

Rhythm Line:

```
secs      .....1.....2.....3.....4.....5.....6.....7.....8.....9....10
120 bpm    1  2  3  4  1  2  3  4  1  2  3  4  1  2  3  4  1  2  3  4
foot       R  L  R  L  L  R  L  R  R  L  R  L  L  R  L  R  Repeat Pattern
```

Cues:

right / behind / right / hitch
left / behind / left / hitch
back / back / back / hitch
step / slide / step / turn

Electric Slide

About this dance: Many people think that the Electric Slide is not a traditional country dance. However, we have found folk-dance references to its basic steps under the name of The Freeze – which is slightly different from The Freeze described in this book. Despite questions about its "authenticity", we have included it for two reasons: it provides an excellent introduction to some basic Country and Western steps, and it is currently being danced to several Country and Western songs.

New Concepts, Steps and Combinations

New Concept

Hand Movements Many dances include arm and hand movements as part of the pattern. Hand and arm movements may accompany foot movements or they may be the only activity choreographed for a sequence of beats. Commonly used arm and hand movements will be defined under "new steps" as they are introduced.

New Steps

Clap Instructs you to clap your hands together, once, on the designated musical beat.

Scuff Instructs you to bring your heel in contact with the floor while you move your foot forward. This will make a noise, and that is important in Country and Western dancing. Scuff sounds are often chosen to accentuate the rhythmic beats in the music to which the dance is done. The scuff involves no weight transfer.

For example, "scuff **left** foot" instructs you to push or scrape your left heel against the floor. In "scuff **left** foot" the right foot supports your weight during and after the scuff.

Touch Instructs you to position your foot at the identified location without a weight transfer. Except when a direction is given to touch with a heel, touches are typically done with the toe of the boot.

For example, "touch **right** foot next to **left** foot" instructs you to bring your right foot next to your left and lightly touch the floor, leaving your right foot ready to move next.

The Dance

Difficulty Level: I
Choreographer: Unknown
Dance Faces: four directions
Pattern Length: 18 Beats
Suggested Music:

For practicing – "I'm So Miserable Without You" – originally recorded by Billy Ray Cyrus (Track 7 on your ***Free CD***).

For dancing – "Fast as You" – originally recorded by Dwight Yoakam (Track 5 on your ***Free CD***). "I Feel Lucky" by Mary Chapin Carpenter.

Beats	Description
	Vines and Claps
1-4	Right vine with left touch and clap
	1 Step **right** foot to right side
	2 Step **left** foot behind **right** foot
	3 Step **right** foot to right side
	4 Touch **left** foot next to **right** foot and clap
5-8	Left vine with right touch
	5 Step **left** foot to left side
	6 Step **right** foot behind **left** foot
	7 Step **left** foot to left side
	8 Touch **right** foot next to **left** foot and clap
	Walk Back and Clap
9	Step **right** foot back
10	Step **left** foot back
11	Step **right** foot back
12	Touch **left** foot next to **right** foot and clap
	Forward and Back and Turn
13	Step **left** foot forward
14	Touch **right** foot next to **left** foot
15	Step **right** foot back
16	Touch **left** foot next to **right** foot
17	Step **left** foot forward
18	Scuff **right** foot and pivot on **left** foot 1/4 turn left

Repeat Pattern

Rhythm Line:

```
secs      .....1.....2.....3.....4.....5.....6.....7.....8.....9....10
120 bpm   1  2  3  4  1  2  3  4  1  2  3  4  1  2  3  4  1  2  3  4
foot      R  L  R  L  L  R  L  R  R  L  R  L  L  R  R  L  L  R  Repeat
```

Cues:

right / behind / right / touch
left / behind / left / touch
back / back / back / touch
step / touch / back / touch
step / turn

Electric Horseman

About this dance: The Electric Horseman is a new Country and Western dance, apparently built upon the Electric Slide. You will see the similarities as you practice the dance. We have also heard this dance referred to as Bartender's Stomp.

New Concepts, Steps and Combinations

New Concept

Syncopated rhythm Most dance steps are choreographed to match full beats of music. On occasion, steps are also choreographed for half-beats. Moving on half versus full beats makes a big difference in the overall look of a dance. In this book, when a dance requires a movement on a half beat, that half beat is labelled with the symbol "&" placed between full beats – "&" should be read as "and".

New Steps

Hold This one is easy. "Hold" instructs you to maintain your position, or do nothing for the designated beats of music.

For example, "hold" means do nothing.

Stomp-up Instructs you to bring the identified foot down with force without a weight transfer to the stomping foot. This will make a noise and, as with scuffs, stomp sounds are often used to accentuate the beats of the music. A "stomp" differs from a "stomp-up" in that in a "stomp" the stomping foot bears weight, but in a "stomp-up", it does not.

For example, "stomp-up **right** foot next to **left** foot" instructs you to bring your right foot down with force next to your left. Your left foot supports your weight during and after the stomp.

The Dance

Difficulty Level: I

Choreographer: Unknown

Dance Faces: four directions

Pattern Length: 24 Beats

Suggested Music:

For practicing – "Talk Some" – originally recorded by Billy Ray Cyrus (Track 3 on your ***Free CD***).

For dancing – "Talk Some" – originally recorded by Billy Ray Cyrus (Track 3 on your ***Free CD***). "I Fought The Law" by Hank Williams, Jr.

Beats	Description
	Vines
1-4	Right vine with left touch
	1 Step **right** foot to right side
	2 Step **left** foot behind **right** foot
	3 Step **right** foot to right side
	4 Touch **left** foot next to **right** foot
5-8	Left vine with right touch
	5 Step **left** foot to left side
	6 Step **right** foot behind **left** foot
	7 Step **left** foot to left side
	8 Touch **right** foot next to **left** foot and clap
	Walk Back
9	Step **right** foot back
10	Step **left** foot back
11	Step **right** foot back
12	Touch **left** foot next to **right** foot
	Steps and Stomp-ups
13	Step **left** foot forward
14	Stomp-up **right** foot next to **left** foot
15	Step **right** foot back
16	Touch **left** foot next to **right** foot
17	Step **left** foot forward
18	Stomp-up **right** foot next to **left** foot
19	Hold
&	Stomp-up **right** foot next to **left** foot
20	Stomp-up **right** foot next to **left** foot
21	Step **right** foot back
22	Touch **left** foot next to **right** foot
23	Step **left** foot forward
24	Scuff **right** foot and pivot on **left** foot 1/4 turn left

Repeat Pattern

Rhythm Line:

```
secs      .....1.....2.....3.....4.....5.....6.....7.....8.....9....10
120 bpm    1  2  3  4  1  2  3  4  1  2  3  4  1  2  3  4  1  2  3 & 4
foot       R  L  R  L  L  R  L  R  R  L  R  L  L  R  R  L  L  R  .R R

secs      ....11....12....13....14....15....16....17....18....19....20
120 bpm    1  2  3  4  1  2  3  4  1  2  3  4  1  2  3  4  1  2  3  4
foot       R  L  L  R  Repeat Pattern
```

Cues:

right / behind / right / touch
left / behind / left / touch
back / back / back / touch
step / stomp / back / touch
step / stomp / hold / stomp-stomp
back / touch / step / turn

The "Hold"

Duchess Hustle

About this dance: This dance is very popular. Its uncomplicated movements make it perfect for slow, "soulful" music.

The Dance

Difficulty Level: I

Choreographer: Unknown

Dance Faces: two directions

Pattern Length: 20 Beats

Suggested Music:

For practicing – "I'm So Miserable Without You" – originally recorded by Billy Ray Cyrus (Track 7 on your ***Free CD***).

For dancing – "I'm So Miserable Without You" – originally recorded by Billy Ray Cyrus (Track 7 on your ***Free CD***). "Black Velvet" by Alannah Myles, "Here in the Real World" by Alan Jackson.

Beats	Description
	Touches and Steps
1	Touch **right** heel forward
2	Touch **right** toe next to **left** foot
3	Touch **right** heel forward
4	Touch **right** toe next to **left** foot
5	Step **right** foot forward
6	Touch **left** heel forward
7	Touch **left** toe to left side
8	Touch **left** toe back
9	Step **left** foot forward
10	Touch **right** heel forward
11	Touch **right** toe to right side
12	Touch **right** toe back
13	Step **right** foot to right side
14	Touch **left** toe behind **right** foot
15	Step **left** foot to left side
16	Touch **right** toe behind **left** foot

Vine with Turn

17-20 Right vine with ½ turn right and left step

- 17 Step **right** foot to right side
- 18 Step **left** foot behind **right** foot
- 19 Step **right** foot to right side and pivot ½ turn right
- 20 Step **left** foot to left side

Repeat Pattern

Rhythm Line:

```
Secs    .....1.....2.....3.....4.....5.....6.....7.....8.....9....10
0 bpm       1   2   3   4   1   2   3   4   1   2   3   4   1   2   3
Foot        R   R   R   R   R   L   L   L   L   R   R   R   R   L   L

Secs    ....11....12....13....14....15....16....17....18....19....20
0 bpm       4   1   2   3   4   1   2   3   4   1   2   3   4   1   2
Foot        R   R   L   R   L   Repeat Pattern
```

Cues:

heel / toe / heel / toe
step / forward / side / back
step / forward / side / back
side / toe / side / toe
right / behind / turn / side

One Step Forward

About this dance: Betty Wilson tells us that the idea for this dance was born in an aisle of a Wal-Mart store in Collinsville, Illinois. Betty encountered a fellow Country and Western dancer in the store and they began talking about One Step Forward, which Desert Rose Band had just released. The two agreed that there should be a special dance to fit that song, particularly since the lyrics promise "a dance like this can never last"! Betty says they worked out a preliminary version of the dance right there in the store. Betty polished it up and now, nine years later, it's danced all over the U.S.

New Concepts, Steps and Combinations

New Steps

Slide-up Instructs you to move the designated foot while keeping it lightly in contact with the floor. This move produces a look of the foot being pulled from one position to the next. When a slide-up is completed, the sliding foot is touching the floor but bears no weight. Note that a slide is different from a slide-up. In a slide, the sliding foot bears weight; in a slide-up, it does not.

For example, "slide-up **right** foot next to **left** foot" instructs you to move your right foot from its last position to a position next to your left foot, while keeping your right foot lightly in contact with the floor.

The Dance

Difficulty Level: I

Choreographer: Betty Wilson

Dance Faces: four directions

Pattern Length: 20 Beats

Suggested Music:

For practicing – "I Wanna Go Too Far" – originally recorded by Trisha Yearwood (Track 4 on your ***Free CD***).

For dancing – "Shut Up And Kiss Me" – originally recorded by Mary Chapin Carpenter (Track 8 on your ***Free CD***). "One Step Forward" by Desert Rose Band.

Beats	Description
	One Step Forward and Two Steps Back
1	Step **left** foot forward
2	Touch **right** foot next to **left** foot
3	Step **right** foot back
4	Step **left** foot next to **right** foot
5	Step **right** foot back
6	Touch **left** foot next to **right** foot
	Side Steps
7	Step **left** foot to left side
8	Step **right** foot next to **left** foot
9	Step **left** foot to left side
10	Touch **right** foot next to **left** foot
	One Step Forward and Two Steps Back
11	Step **right** foot forward
12	Touch **left** foot next to **right** foot
13	Step **left** foot back
14	Step **right** foot next to **left** foot
15	Step **left** foot back
16	Touch **right** foot next to **left** foot
	Side Steps with Turn
17	Step **right** foot to right side
18	Step **left** foot next to **right** foot
19	Step **right** foot to right side
20	Pivot on **right** foot ¼ turn right and touch **left** foot next to **right** foot

Repeat Pattern

Variation

The basic dance involves steps forward, back, and sideways. A variation done in our region changes the forward and backward movements to diagonal movements – taking a liberty with the meaning of the lyrics and certainly an impossibility in the aisles of a store. In addition, some steps are done as slides, and the touches are done as slide-ups. The substitution of slides and slide-ups actually makes the dance a little more difficult because there needs to be more concern about different weight changes on the two different kinds of slide steps that appear in the variation.

Step Slide Forward and Back

1 Step **left** foot diagonally forward
2 Slide-up **right** foot next to **left** foot

3 Step **right** foot diagonally back
4 Slide **left** foot next to **right** foot
5 Step **right** foot diagonally back
6 Slide-up **left** foot next to **right** foot

Step Slides Left

7 Step **left** foot to left side
8 Slide **right** foot next to **left** foot
9 Step **left** foot to left side
10 Slide-up **right** foot next to **left** foot

Step Slide Forward and Back

11 Step **right** foot diagonally forward
12 Slide-up **left** foot next to **right** foot

13 Step **left** foot diagonally back
14 Slide **right** foot next to **left** foot
15 Step **left** foot diagonally back
16 Slide-up **right** foot next to **left** foot

Step Slides Right with Turn

17 Step **right** foot to right side
18 Slide **left** foot next to **right** foot
19 Step **right** foot to right side
20 Pivot on **right** foot 1/4 turn right and touch **left** foot next to **right** foot

Repeat Pattern

Rhythm Line:

```
secs     .....1.....2.....3.....4.....5.....6.....7.....8.....9....10
120 bpm   1  2  3  4  1  2  3  4  1  2  3  4  1  2  3  4  1  2  3  4
foot      L  R  R  L  R  L  L  R  L  R  R  L  L  R  L  R  R  L  R  L
```

Cues:

forward / touch
back / together / back / touch
left / together / left / touch
forward / touch
back / together / back / touch
right / together / right / turn

Cues for variation:

angle / slide
back / slide / back / slide
left / slide / left / slide
angle / slide
back / slide / back / slide
right / slide / right / turn

Kaw-Liga

About this dance: The song after which this dance is named has been around for quite a while. Recorded both by Hank Williams, Sr. and Hank Williams, Jr., it is a popular dance song. The version we usually hear is that recorded by Hank Williams, Sr.

New Concepts, Steps and Combinations

New Steps

Stomp Instructs you to bring the identified foot down with force, transferring weight to the stomping foot. This will make a noise and, as with scuffs, stomp sounds are often used to accentuate the beats of the music. A "stomp" differs from a "stomp-up" in that in a "stomp" the stomping foot bears weight, but in a "stomp-up", it does not.

For example, "stomp **right** foot next to **left** foot" instructs you to bring your right foot down with force next to your left. Your right foot supports all or most of your weight after the stomp.

The Dance

Difficulty Level: I

Choreographer: Unknown

Dance Faces: four directions

Pattern Length: 18 Beats

Suggested Music:

For practicing – "Talk Some" – originally recorded by Billy Ray Cyrus (Track 3 on your ***Free CD***).

For dancing – "Kaw-liga" by Hank Williams, (Jr. or Sr.). "Rodeo" by Garth Brooks

Beats	Description
	Toe Touches
1	Touch **right** toe forward
2	Touch **right** toe to right side
3	Touch **right** toe forward
4	Touch **right** toe to right side

5	Touch **right** toe behind **left** foot
6	Step **right** foot to right side
7	Touch **left** toe behind **right** foot

Vine and Stomps

8-10	Left vine 8 Step **left** foot to left side 9 Step **right** foot behind **left** foot 10 Step **left** foot to left side
11	Stomp-up **right** foot next to **left** foot
12	Stomp-up **right** foot next to **left** foot

Hitches and Turn

13	Step **right** foot back
14	Hitch **left** leg
15	Step **left** foot forward
16	Hitch **right** leg and pivot on **left** foot $1/4$ turn left
17	Stomp **right** foot next to **left** foot
18	Hold

Repeat Pattern

Rhythm Line:

```
secs      .....1.....2.....3.....4.....5.....6.....7.....8.....9....10
120 bpm    1  2  3  4  1  2  3  4  1  2  3  4  1  2  3  4  1  2  3  4
foot       R  R  R  R  R  R  L  L  R  L  R  R  R  L  L  R  R  .  Repeat
```

Cues:

toe forward / side / forward / side
toe back / step right / toe back
left / behind / left
stomp / stomp
back / hitch / left / turn
stomp / hold

Cowboy Boogie

About this dance: This dance appears to have been around for a while. As it has moved from place to place, it has undergone some variations and acquired new names. Sometimes this dance is called Charleston Rock, Watergate or Ming Boogie. In some places it is danced with hitches or kicks instead of scuffs.

New Concepts, Steps and Combinations

New Steps

Bump Gives you an instruction for hip movement independent of foot movement. Bump instructs you to move your hips, once, on the designated musical beat. The hip that moves out (right or left) and the direction of the bump (for example, forward or backward) will be specified in the dance description. In a bump, your weight is supported by both feet. Bumps are generally easier to execute if the knees are bent slightly.

For example, "bump **right** hip to the right" instructs you to move your right hip to the right on the beat of music.

Rock Instructs you to move your body in the direction specified, over the foot that is in that location. The instruction, "rock", refers to movement of the body, and not the feet. If the dancer needs to move the foot in order to execute the body movement, the term "rock-step" is used. A rock is easier to execute if the knees are bent slightly.

For example, "rock forward on **right** foot" instructs you to move, or rock, your body forward, over your right foot.

The Dance

Difficulty Level: I
Choreographer: Unknown
Dance Faces: four directions
Pattern Length: 24 Beats
Suggested Music:

For practicing – "The City Put The Country Back In Me" – originally recorded by Neal McCoy (Track 2 on your ***Free CD***).

For dancing – "Fast as You" – originally recorded by Dwight Yoakam (Track 5 on your ***Free CD***). "The South's Gonna Do It" – originally recorded by Charlie Daniels Band (Track 6 on your ***Free CD***). "Cowboy Boogie" by Randy Travis.

Beats	**Description**
	Vines and Scuffs
1-4	Right vine with left scuff
	1 Step **right** foot to right side
	2 Step **left** foot behind **right** foot
	3 Step **right** foot to right side
	4 Scuff **left** foot
5-8	Left vine with right scuff
	5 Step **left** foot to left side
	6 Step **right** foot behind **left** foot
	7 Step **left** foot to left side
	8 Scuff **right** foot
	Forward and Scuff
9	Step **right** foot forward
10	Scuff **left** foot
11	Step **left** foot forward
12	Scuff **right** foot
	Back and Hitch
13	Step **right** foot back
14	Step **left** foot back
15	Step **right** foot back
16	Hitch **left** leg
	Hip Bumps and Turn
17	Step **left** foot diagonally forward and bump **left** hip diagonally forward
18	Bump **left** hip diagonally forward
19	Bump **right** hip diagonally back
20	Bump **right** hip diagonally back
21	Rock forward on **left** foot
22	Rock back on **right** foot
23	Rock forward on **left** foot
24	Hitch **right** leg and pivot on **left** foot 1/4 turn to the left

Repeat Pattern

Variations

A. Substitute hitches (or kicks) for scuffs on steps 4, 8, 10, and 12.

B. Change the simple bumps and rocks on steps 17-24 to bumps in a syncopated rhythm. That is, substitute the following:

	Hip Bumps and Turn
17	Step **left** foot diagonally forward and bump **left** hip diagonally forward
&	Bump **right** hip diagonally back
18	Bump **left** hip diagonally forward
19	Bump **right** hip diagonally back
&	Bump **left** hip diagonally forward
20	Bump **right** hip diagonally back
21	Bump **left** hip diagonally forward
22	Bump **right** hip diagonally back
23	Bump **left** hip diagonally forward
24	Hitch **right** leg and pivot on **left** foot 1/4 turn to the left

Rhythm, Line:

```
secs      .....1.....2.....3.....4.....5.....6.....7.....8.....9....10
120 bpm    1  2  3  4  1  2  3  4  1  2  3  4  1  2  3  4  1  2  3  4
foot       R  L  R  L  L  R  L  R  R  L  L  R  R  L  R  L  L  .  .  .
other                                                      b  b  b  b
                                                           (bumps)

secs      ....11....12....13....14....15....16....17....18....19....20
120 bpm    1  2  3  4  1  2  3  4  1  2  3  4  1  2  3  4  1  2  3  4
foot       L  R  L  R    Repeat Pattern
other
```

Variation

```
secs      .....1.....2.....3.....4.....5.....6.....7.....8.....9....10
120 bpm    1  2  3  4  1  2  3  4  1  2  3  4  1  2  3  4  1 & 2  3 & 4
foot       R  L  R  L  L  R  L  R  R  L  L  R  R  L  R  L  L  .  .  .
other                                                      b b b  b b b
                                                          (bumps)

secs      ....11....12....13....14....15....16....17....18....19....20
120 bpm    1  2  3  4  1  2  3  4  1  2  3  4  1  2  3  4  1  2  3  4
foot       .  .  .  R    Repeat Pattern
other      b  b  b
           (bumps)
```

Cues:

right / behind / right / scuff
left / behind / left / scuff
forward / scuff / forward / scuff
back / back / back / hitch
bump / bump / bump / bump
rock forward / back / forward / turn

Macarena

About this dance: Macarena is choreographed to accompany a song of the same name by Los Del Rio. Unlike many other line dances, Macarena is comprised mainly of hand movements. Macarena, the song, is an example of Tejano music. A musical style begun in South-western Texas, Tejano music reflects a blend of Mexican and Country and Western musical styles. Using instruments typically found in Mexican music, Tejano songs often tell stories, as Country and Western music does. The lyrics are most often in Spanish.

Following the dance description, we suggest some variations for you to try. We refrain, however, from offering a variation we saw performed at the 1996 Olympics by the U.S. Women's Gymnastic Team: in place of the paddle turn on beats 13-16, they did back flips!

New Concepts, Steps and Combinations

New Concept

Latin- "Latin-" is used as a prefix with a variety of steps and instructs you to sway your hips in the direction of the moving foot. This sway is a fluid movement of the hips from one location to the next and is unlike the bump, which is sharp and pronounced.

For example, " Latin-step **left** foot to left side" instructs you to step to the left, swaying your left hip to the left as you take the step.

New Combinations

Paddle Turn Instructs you to make a turn while you alternate weight from your "anchor" foot (the foot in the direction of the turn) to your "paddle" foot. In a paddle turn you will make a series of small turns in order to complete a 1/4, 1/2, 3/4 or full turn. Each small turn will begin by stepping the "anchor" foot in place but toward the direction of the turn. The "paddling" foot will next step to a position parallel to the anchor foot and about shoulder width apart. The paddle turn has the look of a boat going around in a circle as it is paddled with one oar. The number of beats it will take to execute the turn, the total amount of the turn and the direction of the paddle turn will be specified in the dance description.

For example, "beats 1- 4 1/4 Paddle turn to the left" instructs you to: on beat one, step your left foot in place and turned out (i.e. pointed diagonally left); on beat two, step your right foot parallel to your left foot, about shoulder width apart (completing a 1/8 turn to the left); on beat three, step your left foot in place and turned out; and on beat four, step your right foot parallel to your left, about shoulder width apart (completing another 1/8 turn to the left).

The Dance

Difficulty Level: I

Choreographer: Unknown

Dance Faces: four directions

Pattern Length: 16 Beats

Suggested Music:

For practicing – "Talk Some" – originally recorded by Billy Ray Cyrus (Track 3 on your ***Free CD***).

For dancing – "Macarena" by Los Del Rio.

Beats	Description
	Hand Moves
1	Latin-step **left** foot in place and extend right arm forward, palm down
2	Latin-step **right** foot in place and extend left arm forward, palm down
3	Latin-step **left** foot in place and turn right palm up (arm remains extended)
4	Latin-step **right** foot in place and turn left palm up (arm remains extended)
5	Latin-step **left** foot in place and place right hand on left upper arm
6	Latin-step **right** foot in place and place left hand on right upper arm
7	Latin-step **left** foot in place and place right hand at nape of neck, right side
8	Latin-step **right** foot in place and place left hand at nape of neck, left side
9	Latin-step **left** foot in place and place right hand on side of left hip
10	Latin-step **right** foot in place and place left hand on side of right hip
11	Latin-step **left** foot in place and place right hand on back of right hip
12	Latin-step **right** foot in place and place left hand on back of left hip
	Latin-Paddle Turn
13-16	¼ Latin-paddle turn to the left
	13 Latin-step **left** foot *(turned out)* in place
	14 Latin-step **right** foot next to **left** foot
	15 Latin-step **left** foot *(turned out)* in place
	16 Latin-step **right** foot next to **left** foot

Repeat Pattern

Variation

1. Some dancers do the 4 beat ¼ Latin-paddle turn in double time. This means that instead of moving on each of four beats, they move on every beat and every half-beat from beat 13 through beat 16. Instead of doing ⅛ turns on beats 13 and 15 and stepping the right foot on beats 14 and 16, they do $\frac{1}{16}$ turns on 13, 14, 15 and 16 and step the right foot on the half-beats after each of those four beats.

2. Some dancers jump forward and clap on the last beat of the turn.

3. Some dancers replace the Latin-paddle turn with three Latin-steps in place (left, right, left) followed by a ¼ turn left while jumping forward and clapping.

Rhythm Line:

```
secs      .....1.....2.....3.....4.....5.....6.....7.....8.....9....10
120 bpm    1  2  3  4  1  2  3  4  1  2  3  4  1  2  3  4  1  2  3  4
foot       L  R  L  R  L  R  L  R  L  R  L  R  L  R  L  R  Repeat Pattern
other      h  h  h  h  h  h  h  h  h  h  h  h
          (hand movements - alternating right, left)
```

Cues:

palm down / down / up / up
arm / arm / neck / neck
hip / hip / back / back
turn / sway / turn / sway

A COWBOY GETTING UP THE COURAGE TO ADD A BACK FLIP TO HIS "MACARENA"

Chattahoochee

About this dance: The popularity of Country and Western dancing has grown tremendously since the late 1980s. These days it is common for a new dance to be choreographed to accompany a Country and Western song that becomes popular. The Chattahoochee is one of those dances. While you will enjoy dancing it to "Chattahoochee" by Alan Jackson, also try dancing it to other songs of similar rhythm, tempo and mood.

New Concepts, Steps and Combinations

New Concepts

Weighted leg Refers to the leg supporting the weight of the body.

New Steps

Hook Instructs you to bend your knee, raise your leg, and cross it in front of or behind the weighted leg. The leg to be hooked, and whether it crosses in front of or behind the weighted leg will be specified in the step description. The hooked leg crosses the weighted leg slightly below knee level. The foot of the hooked leg should be turned out. This movement is done in one beat of music. On occasion, a step description will instruct you to hook your leg to the side. In a hook to the side, the hooked leg will angle out to the side and the toe will point down.

For example, "hook **right** leg across **left** leg" instructs you to bend the knee of your right leg, lifting it off the floor, and to cross your right leg in front of your left leg. Your right foot should be turned out.

Slap Instructs you to slap your foot (or other identified body part). The instruction will identify the slapping hand and the body part. The left hand always slaps the left side of the designated parts and the right hand slaps the right side.

Swivel heels Instructs you to turn both heels in the direction specified (i.e. left, right or center). Movement is executed by supporting the weight on the balls of both feet and turning the heels approximately 45 degrees in the direction indicated. While your feet move in this step, your body continues to face forward. Note that a "swivel" is different from a "twist" in which your body would be allowed to move with your feet. Note also, "swivel heels" (in which your heels are turned) is different from "swivel toes" (in which your toes are turned.)

For example, "swivel heels to left" instructs you to put your body weight over the balls of both feet and turn your heels to the left. Note that when you complete this move, your toes will be pointed to the right. "Swivel heels to center" instructs you to return your heels to their starting position under your body.

New Combinations

Boot hook combination Instructs you to make a sequence of four movements, one of which will be a hook, in four beats of music. The four movements are executed by the identified leg, while the other leg supports the weight of the body. On beat one, the heel will touch diagonally forward, with foot turned out. On beat two, the foot is hooked in front of the weighted leg. On beat three, the heel is touched diagonally forward, with foot turned out. On beat four, the foot steps next to the weighted foot.

For example, "left boot hook combination" instructs you to: on one, touch your left heel, with foot turned out, diagonally forward; on two, hook your left leg in front of your right leg; on three, touch your left heel, with foot turned out, diagonally forward; and on four, step your left foot next to your right.

The Dance

Difficulty Level: I

Choreographer: Unknown

Dance Faces: four directions

Pattern Length: 28 Beats

Suggested Music:

For practicing – "I Wanna Go Too Far" – originally recorded by Kathy Mattea (Track 4 on your ***Free CD***).

For dancing – "Redneck Girl" – originally recorded by Bellamy Brothers (Track 11 on your ***Free CD***). "Chattahoochee" by Alan Jackson

---

Beats	Description
	Boot Hooks and Swivels
1-4	Left boot hook combination
	1 Touch **left** heel *(foot turned out)* diagonally forward
	2 Hook **left** leg *(foot turned out)* in front of **right** leg
	3 Touch **left** heel *(foot turned out)* diagonally forward
	4 Step **left** foot next to **right** foot
5	Swivel heels to left
6	Swivel heels to center
7	Swivel heels to left
8	Swivel heels to center
9 -12	Right boot hook combination
	9 Touch **right** heel *(foot turned out)* diagonally forward
	10 Hook **right** leg *(foot turned out)* in front of **left** leg
	11 Touch **right** heel *(foot turned out)* diagonally forward
	12 Step **right** foot next to **left** foot

13 Swivel heels right
14 Swivel heels center
15 Swivel heels right
16 Swivel heels center

Slaps

17 Step **right** foot to right side
18 Hook **left** leg behind **right** leg and slap **left** heel with right hand
19 Step **left** foot to left side
20 Hook **right** leg behind **left** leg and slap **right** heel with left hand

Vine and Turn

21-24 Right vine with left hitch and $\frac{1}{4}$ turn right
- 21 Step **right** foot to right side
- 22 Step **left** foot behind **right** foot
- 23 Step **right** foot to right side
- 24 Hitch **left** foot and pivot on **right** foot $\frac{1}{4}$ turn right

Walk Back

25 Step **left** foot back
26 Step **right** foot back
27 Step **left** foot back
28 Stomp **right** foot next to **left** foot

Repeat Pattern

Rhythm Line:

```
secs     .....1.....2.....3.....4.....5.....6.....7.....8.....9....10
120 bpm    1  2  3  4  1  2  3  4  1  2  3  4  1  2  3  4  1  2  3  4
foot       L  L  L  L  B  B  B  B  R  R  R  R  B  B  B  B  R  L  L  R
other                                                         s     s
                                                           (slap)

secs     ....11....12....13....14....15....16....17....18....19....20
120 bpm    1  2  3  4  1  2  3  4  1  2  3  4  1  2  3  4  1  2  3  4
foot       R  L  R  L  L  R  L  R  Repeat Pattern
other
```

Cues:

left heel / hook / heel / together
left / center / left / center
right heel / hook / heel / together
right / center / right / center
right / slap / left / slap
right / behind / right / turn
back / back / back / stomp

Sleazy Slide

New Concepts, Steps and Combinations

New Steps

Draw

Instructs you to slide the identified foot for a designated number of beats. The action is continuous, but slow. This move produces a look of the foot being pulled from one position to the next. At the conclusion of a draw, most or all of the body weight is supported by the drawn foot. A draw is similar in movement to a slide; they differ only in that a slide is completed in one beat of music. Note that a draw is different from a draw-up. In a draw, the sliding foot bears weight; in a draw-up, it does not.

For example, "for beats 1-3, draw **left** foot next to **right** foot" specifies a three beat draw of the left foot. On beat one, you would begin to slide your left foot toward your right, and you would continue this motion through beat two. On beat three, the draw is completed with most or all of your weight transferred to your left foot.

Rock-step

Instructs you to step in the direction specified, but, unlike a simple "step", it requires you to lean your body in the direction of the step. If the dancer does not need to move the foot in order to execute the body movement, the term "rock" is used. A rock-step is easier to execute if the knees are bent slightly.

For example, "rock-step **left** foot back" instructs you to step back on your left foot and lean your body slightly back, over your left foot, as you take this step.

New Combinations

Military Turn

Instructs you to make a 180 degree (½) turn in two beats of music. The direction of the turn (right or left) will always be specified. On beat one, the foot opposite the direction of the turn steps forward. On beat two, the body makes a ½ turn in the direction specified, pivoting on the balls of both feet. A "military turn" includes only one instruction for a change of foot location, at the close of a military turn the dancer will be standing with one foot in front of the other.

For example, "military turn to the left" instructs you to, on beat one, step forward on your right foot and, on beat two, pivot ½ turn left on the balls of both feet. At the close of a "military turn to the left" the dancer will be standing with feet separated and with the right foot behind the left.

The Dance

Difficulty Level: I

Choreographer: Unknown

Dance Faces: four directions

Pattern Length: 24 Beats

Suggested Music:

For practicing – "I'm So Miserable Without You" – originally recorded by Billy Ray Cyrus (Track 7 on your ***Free CD***).

For dancing – "Shut Up And Kiss Me" – originally recorded by Mary Chapin Carpenter (Track 8 on your ***Free CD***). "Super Love" by Exile.

Beats	Description
	Step and Draw
1	Step **right** foot to right side
2-3	Draw **left** foot next to **right** foot
4	Clap
5	Step **right** foot to right side
6-7	Draw **left** foot next to **right** foot
8	Clap
9	Step **left** foot to left side
10-11	Draw **right** foot next to **left** foot
12	Clap
	Rock Steps
13	Rock-step **right** foot forward
14	Rock back on **left** foot
15	Rock-step **right** foot back
16	Rock forward on **left** foot
	Turns
17-18	Military turn to the left
	17 Step **right** foot forward
	18 Pivot on **both** feet ½ turn left
19-20	Military turn to the left
	19 Step **right** foot forward
	20 Pivot on **both** feet ½ turn left
21	Step **right** foot forward
22	Pivot on **both** feet ¼ turn left
23	Stomp **right** foot next to **left** foot
24	Clap

Repeat Pattern

Variation

Some dancers like to add shoulder shimmies to the step and draw movements at beats 1-3, 5-7, and 9-11.

Rhythm Line:

```
secs      .....1.....2.....3.....4.....5.....6.....7.....8.....9....10
120 bpm    1  2  3  4  1  2  3  4  1  2  3  4  1  2  3  4  1  2  3  4
foot       R  - L-  .  R  - L-  .  L  - R-  .  R  L  R  L  R  B  R  B
other               c           c           c
                  (clap)
```

```
secs      ....11....12....13....14....15....16....17....18....19....20
120 bpm    1  2  3  4  1  2  3  4  1  2  3  4  1  2  3  4  1  2  3  4
foot       R  B  R  .  Repeat Pattern
other               c
```

Cues:

right / draw / draw / clap
right / draw / draw / clap
left / draw / draw / clap
rock forward / back / back / forward
right / turn / step / turn
step / turn / stomp / clap

Yankee Shuffle

About this dance: This line dance appears to have been around for a while. With its easy, sliding style it's a good dance for tired dancers who are not ready to call it a night!

New Concepts, Steps and Combinations

New Steps

Brush Instructs you to move the specified foot by gently moving the ball of the foot across the floor. Brushes are most often done forward, but the direction will be specified in the dance description. This movement is much like a "scuff", except that in a "scuff" the heel comes in contact with the floor (and makes considerable noise), whereas in a "brush", the ball of the foot is in contact with the floor (and produces much less noise). The brush involves no weight transfer.

For example, "brush **left** foot forward" instructs you to gently move the ball of the left foot forward across the floor. In "brush **left** foot forward" the right foot supports your weight during and after the brush.

The Dance

Difficulty Level: I

Choreographer: Unknown

Dance Faces: four directions

Pattern Length: 20 Beats

Suggested Music:

For practicing – "Wher'm I Gonna Live When I Get Home" – originally recorded by Billy Ray Cyrus (Track 9 on your ***Free CD***).

For dancing – "Wher'm I Gonna Live When I Get Home" – originally recorded by Billy Ray Cyrus (Track 9 on your ***Free CD***). "Fast as You" – originally recorded by Dwight Yoakam (Track 5 on your ***Free CD***). "Jukebox with a Country Song" by Doug Stone.

Beats	Description
	Vine and Turn
1-4	Right vine with left brush and $1/4$ turn right
	1 Step **right** foot to right side
	2 Step **left** foot behind **right** foot
	3 Step **right** foot to right side
	4 Brush **left** foot forward and pivot on **right** foot $1/4$ turn right

Rock and Turn and Rock

5 Rock-step **left** foot forward
6 Rock back on **right** foot
7 Rock forward on **left** foot
8 Brush **right** foot forward and pivot on **left** foot ½ turn left

9 Rock-step **right** foot forward
10 Rock back on **left** foot
11 Rock forward on **right** foot
12 Brush **left** foot forward

Step and Brush

13 Step **left** foot forward
14 Brush **right** foot forward
15 Step **right** foot forward
16 Brush **left** foot forward

Vine

17-20 Left vine with right brush
- 17 Step **left** foot to left side
- 18 Step **right** foot behind **left** foot
- 19 Step **left** foot to left side
- 20 Brush **right** foot forward

Repeat Pattern

Rhythm Line:

```
secs      .....1.....2.....3.....4.....5.....6.....7.....8.....9....10
120 bpm    1  2  3  4  1  2  3  4  1  2  3  4  1  2  3  4  1  2  3  4
foot       R  L  R  L  L  R  L  R  R  L  R  L  L  R  R  L  L  R  L  R
```

Cues:

right / behind / right / turn
rock forward / back / forward / turn
rock forward / back / forward / brush
left / brush / right / brush
left / behind / right / brush

Flying Eight

About this dance: In some places, this dance is called Flying Eight, in others, Flying Eights. We have no idea why. It is done as a drill line dance and as a contra dance. We have seen several different descriptions of this dance, with different turns on different beats. We present the version done in our region.

The Dance

Difficulty Level: I

Choreographer: Unknown

Dance Faces: two directions

Pattern Length: 18 Beats

Suggested Music:

For practicing – "I'm So Miserable Without You" – originally recorded by Billy Ray Cyrus (Track 7 on your ***Free CD***).

For dancing – "The City Put The Country Back In Me" – originally recorded by Neal McCoy (Track 2 on your ***Free CD***). "Walkin' Away A Winner" – originally recorded by Kathy Mattea (Track 1 on your ***Free CD***).

Beats	Description
	Vines
1-4	Left vine with right hitch 1 Step **left** foot to left side 2 Step **right** foot behind **left** foot 3 Step **left** foot to left side 4 Hitch **right** leg
5-8	Right vine with 1/4 turn right and left hitch 5 Step **right** foot to right side 6 Step **left** foot behind **right** foot 7 Step **right** foot to right side and pivot 1/4 turn right 8 Hitch **left** leg
9-12	Left vine with 3/4 turn left and right hitch 9 Step **left** foot to left side 10 Step **right** foot behind **left** foot 11 Step **left** foot to left side 12 Hitch **right** leg and pivot on **left** foot 3/4 turn left

Steps and Hitches

13	Step **right** foot forward
14	Hitch **left** leg
15	Step **left** foot forward
16	Hitch **right** leg
17	Step **right** foot forward
18	Hitch **left** leg

Repeat Pattern

Rhythm Line:

```
secs      .....1.....2.....3.....4.....5.....6.....7.....8.....9....10
120 bpm    1  2  3  4  1  2  3  4  1  2  3  4  1  2  3  4  1  2  3  4
foot       L  R  L  R  R  L  R  L  L  R  L  R  R  L  L  R  R  L Repeat
```

Cues:

left / behind / left / hitch
right / behind / turn / hitch
left / behind / left / turn
forward / hitch / forward / hitch
forward / hitch

Level II

Funky Cowboy

New Combination

Shuffle Instructs you to make three steps, in a specified order, to two beats of music. The direction of the shuffle (forward, backward, or to the side) and the foot that begins, or leads, the shuffle, will be specified in the dance description. On the first beat of music in a shuffle, the leading foot steps in the direction specified. On the half beat, the ball of the following foot steps next to the heel of the leading foot. On the second beat of music, the leading foot again steps in the specified direction. In a shuffle, feet are gently dragged or barely lifted from position to position.

For example, "right shuffle forward" instructs you to step forward on your right foot, step the ball of your left foot next to heel of your right foot, and step forward on your right foot, to a rhythm of "one-and-two".

The Dance

Difficulty Level: II

Choreographer: Unknown

Dance Faces: two directions

Pattern Length: 32 Beats

Suggested Music:

For practicing – "Wher'm I Gonna Live When I Get Home" – originally recorded by Billy Ray Cyrus (Track 9 on your ***Free CD***).

For dancing – "Fast as You" – originally recorded by Dwight Yoakam (Track 5 on your ***Free CD***). "Dancin' Cowboy" by Bellamy Brothers.

Beats	Description
	Toe Touches and Vines
1	Touch **right** toe to right side
2	Touch **right** toe behind **left** foot
3	Touch **right** toe to right side
4	Touch **right** toe behind **left** foot
5- 8	Right vine with left touch
	5 Step **right** foot to right side
	6 Step **left** foot behind **right** foot
	7 Step **right** foot to right side
	8 Touch **left** foot next to **right** foot
9	Touch **left** toe to left side
10	Touch **left** toe behind **right** foot
11	Touch **left** toe to left side
12	Touch **left** toe behind **right** foot

13-16 Left vine with right touch
- 13 Step **left** foot to left side
- 14 Step **right** foot behind **left** foot
- 15 Step **left** foot to left side
- 16 Touch **right** foot next to **left** foot

Hip Bumps

17 Step **right** foot diagonally forward and bump **right** hip diagonally forward
18 Bump **right** hip diagonally forward
19 Bump **left** hip diagonally back
20 Bump **left** hip diagonally back

21 Bump **right** hip diagonally forward
22 Bump **left** hip diagonally back
23 Bump **right** hip diagonally forward
24 Bump **left** hip diagonally back

Shuffles

25-26 Right shuffle forward
- 25 Step **right** foot forward
- & Step **left** foot next to **right** foot
- 26 Step **right** foot forward

27-28 Left shuffle forward
- 27 Step **left** foot forward
- & Step **right** foot next to **left** foot
- 28 Step **left** foot forward

Turn and Walk

29 Pivot on **left** foot ½ turn to right and step **right** foot next to **left** foot
30 Step **left** foot forward
31 Step **right** foot forward
32 Step **left** foot forward

Repeat Pattern

Rhythm Line:

```
secs      .....1.....2.....3.....4.....5.....6.....7.....8.....9....10
120 bpm     1   2   3   4   1   2   3   4   1   2   3   4   1   2   3   4   1   2   3   4
foot        R   R   R   R   R   L   R   L   L   L   L   L   L   R   L   R   R   .   .   .
other                                                                       b   b   b   b
                                                                            (hip bumps)

secs      ....11....12....13....14....15....16....17....18....19....20
120 bpm     1   2   3   4   1 & 2  3 & 4   1   2   3   4   1   2   3   4   1   2   3   4
foot        .   .   .   .   R L R  L R L   R   L   R   L    Repeat Pattern
other       b   b   b   b
```

Cues:

toe / behind / toe / behind
right / behind / right / touch
toe / behind / toe / behind
left / behind / left / touch
bump forward / forward / back / back
bump forward / back / forward / back
right - together - right / left - together - left
turn / left / right / left

Cowgirls' Twist

About this dance: Cowgirls' Twist is a new dance that many cowboys (i.e. Tony) think is too feminine for them to do. But many other cowboys like to do this dance – so give it a try. This dance involves a different kind of pivot move: on beat 31, you pivot on the *heel* of one foot and the *ball* of the other. This move will be easier if you take a small step forward on beat 29.

New Concepts, Steps and Combinations

New Steps

Swivel toes Instructs you to turn both toes in the direction specified (left, right or center). Movement is executed by supporting the weight on the heels of both feet and turning the toes approximately 45 degrees in the direction indicated. While your feet move in this step, your body continues to face forward. Note that a "swivel" is different from a "twist" in which your body would be allowed to move with your feet. Note also that toe swivels differ from heel swivels in which you move your heels while supporting your weight on your toes.

For example, "swivel toes to left" instructs you to put your body weight over the heels of both feet and turn your toes to the left. Note that when you complete this move, your toes will be pointed to the left. "Swivel toes to center" instructs you to return your toes to their starting position under your body.

New Combination

Heel Strut Instructs you to execute two moves in two beats of music. The foot involved in the strut, will be specified in the dance description. On beat one, the heel of the specified foot is touched forward with the toe pointing up. On beat two, the toe of the specified foot is lowered as weight is transferred to that foot. Unlike toe struts, heel struts are always done moving forward.

For example, "left heel strut" instructs you, on beat one, to touch your left heel forward, and on beat two, to lower your left toe to the floor and step down.

The Dance

Difficulty Level: II

Choreographer: Bill Bader

Dance Faces: four directions

Pattern Length: 32 Beats

Suggested Music:

For practicing – "Talk Some" – originally recorded by Billy Ray Cyrus (Track 3 on your ***Free CD***).

For dancing – "The South's Gonna Do It" – originally recorded by Charlie Daniels Band (Track 6 on your ***Free CD***). "What The Cowgirls Do" by Vince Gill.

Beats	Description
	Heel Struts
1- 2	Right heel strut
	1 Touch **right** heel forward
	2 Lower **right** toe (step **right** foot down)
3- 4	Left heel strut
	3 Touch **left** heel forward
	4 Lower **left** toe (step **left** foot down)
5- 6	Right heel strut
	5 Touch **right** heel forward
	6 Lower **right** toe (step **right** foot down)
7- 8	Left heel strut
	7 Touch **left** heel forward
	8 Lower **left** toe (step **left** foot down)
	Walk Back
9	Step **right** foot back
10	Step **left** foot back
11	Step **right** foot back
12	Step **left** foot next to **right** foot
	Swive to Left
13	Swivel heels to left
14	Swivel toes to left
15	Swivel heels to left
16	Hold (clap optional)
	Swivel to Right
17	Swivel heels to right
18	Swivel toes to right
19	Swivel heels to right
20	Hold (clap optional)

Heel Swivels

21 Swivel heels to left
22 Hold (clap optional)
23 Swivel heels to right
24 Hold (clap optional)

Heel Swivels and Hold

25 Swivel heels to left
26 Swivel heels to right
27 Swivel heels to center
28 Hold

Step and Turn

29 Step **right** foot forward
30 Hold
31 Rock back on left foot and pivot on heel of **left** foot and ball of **right** foot 1/4 turn left
32 Hold

Repeat Pattern

Rhythm Line:

```
secs     .....1.....2.....3.....4.....5.....6.....7.....8.....9....10
90 bpm      1    2    3    4    1    2    3    4    1    2    3    4    1    2    3
foot        R    R    L    L    R    R    L    L    R    L    R    L    B    B    B
other

secs     ....11....12....13....14....15....16....17....18....19....20
90 bpm      4    1    2    3    4    1    2    3    4    1    2    3    4    1    2
foot        .    B    B    B    .    B    .    B    .    B    B    B    .    R    .
other       c                   c         c         c
         (clap optional)

secs     ....21....22....23....24....25....26....27....28....29....30
90 bpm      3    4    1    2    3    4    1    2    3    4    1    2    3    4    1
foot        B    .    Repeat Pattern
other
```

Cues:

right heel / step / heel / step
heel / step / heel / step
back right / left / right / together
heels left / toes / heels / clap
heels right / toes / heels / clap
heels left / clap / heels right / clap
heels left / right / center / hold
forward / hold / turn / hold

East Coast Swing Line Dance

About this dance: This dance seems oddly named, to us, as it does not use the side step and rock step patterns used in the couples dance style called "east coast swing". Nevertheless, East Coast Swing Line Dance is fun to do.

The Dance

Difficulty Level: II

Choreographer: Unknown

Dance Faces: four directions

Pattern Length: 32 Beats

Suggested Music:

For practicing – "I Wanna Go Too Far" – originally recorded by Trisha Yearwood (Track 4 on your ***Free CD***).

For dancing – "Shut Up And Kiss Me" – originally recorded by Mary Chapin Carpenter (Track 8 on your ***Free CD***). "Honky Tonk Walkin'" by Kentucky Headhunters.

Beats	Description
	Touches
1	Touch **right** heel forward
2	Touch **right** toe next to **left** foot
3	Touch **right** toe back
4	Step **right** foot next to **left** foot
5	Touch **left** heel forward
6	Touch **left** toe next to **right** foot
7	Touch **left** toe back
8	Touch **left** foot next to **right** foot next to **left** foot
	Vines
9-12	Left vine with right stomp-up
	9 Step **left** foot to left side
	10 Step **right** foot behind **left** foot
	11 Step **left** foot to left side
	12 Stomp-up **right** foot next to **left** foot

13-16 Right vine with left stomp-up
- 13 Step **right** foot to right side
- 14 Step **left** foot behind **right** foot
- 15 Step **right** foot to right side
- 16 Stomp-up **left** foot next to **left** foot

Forward Steps and Slides

17 Step **left** foot forward
18 Slide **right** foot next to **left** foot
19 Step **left** foot forward
20 Scuff **right** foot

21 Step **right** foot forward
22 Slide **left** foot next to **right** foot
23 Step **right** foot forward
24 Touch **left** foot next to **right** foot

Vine and Turn

25-28 Left vine with 1/4 turn left and right step
- 25 Step **left** foot to left side
- 26 Step **right** foot behind **left** foot
- 27 Step **left** foot to left side and pivot 1/4 turn left
- 28 Step **right** foot next to **left** foot

Heel Swivels

29 Swivel heels to right
30 Swivel heels to center
31 Swivel heels to left
32 Swivel heels to center

Repeat Pattern

Rhythm Line:

```
secs     .....1.....2.....3.....4.....5.....6.....7.....8.....9....10
120 bpm    1  2  3  4  1  2  3  4  1  2  3  4  1  2  3  4  1  2  3  4
foot       R  R  R  R  L  L  L  L  L  R  L  R  R  L  R  L  L  R  L  R

secs     ....11....12....13....14....15....16....17....18....19....20
120 bpm    1  2  3  4  1  2  3  4  1  2  3  4  1  2  3  4  1  2  3  4
foot       R  L  R  L  L  R  L  R  B  B  B  B  Repeat Pattern
```

Cues:

right heel / together / toe back / together
left heel / together / toe back / together
left / behind / left / stomp
right / behind / right / stomp
forward / slide / forward / scuff
forward / slide / forward / touch
left / behind / turn / together
heels right / center / left / center

Boot Scootin' Boogie II

About this dance: There are many dances called Boot Scootin' Boogie, all choreographed to the song Boot Scootin' Boogie by Brooks and Dunn. Needless to say, these are relatively new dances. The "Boot Scootin' Boogie" described here is the one we enjoy doing. There really is no "scootin'" in either this dance or in Boot Scootin' Boogie I. Scoots will be found, however, in Slappin' Leather, along with some leather slapping.

New Concepts, Steps and Combinations

New Steps

Chug Instructs you to bend the knee of the leg specified and lift the leg slightly from the floor. This move is very much like a "hitch". The difference is one of degree. While in a hitch the thigh is nearly parallel to the floor, a chug is a much smaller move. In a chug, the foot is lifted only a few inches from the floor. For example, "chug **left** leg" instructs you to bend your left knee as you lift your left foot slightly off the floor.

Kick Instructs you to kick the specified foot about half-way between the floor and knee-height. Kicks are most often done forward, but the direction of the kick will be specified in the step instruction. In country dancing, kicks are done with the toes pointing up, as if to shake *something* off the boot.

Twist Instructs you to turn your body without lifting your feet from the floor. The direction of the twist (diagonally right or diagonally left) will be specified. Often, after a series of twists, "twist center" will instruct you to return your body to a forward facing position. Twists are easier to execute if the knees are bent slightly and the weight is over the balls of the feet, not the heels.

For example, "twist left" instructs you to turn your body diagonally left by supporting your weight on the balls of your feet and moving your heels to the right.

New Combination

Kick-Ball-Change Instructs you to make three steps, in a specified order, to two beats of music. The foot that begins or leads the kick-ball-change will be specified in the dance description. On the first beat of a kick-ball-change, the leading foot is kicked forward (about six inches off the floor). On the half beat, the ball of the leading foot steps next to the following foot. On the second beat, the following foot steps in place. The dancer should note that this third movement is subtle. The following foot has not moved: it has simply stepped in place. An alternative way to think of this third movement is as a transfer of body weight from the leading foot to the following foot.

For example, "right kick-ball-change" instructs you to kick your right foot forward, step the ball of your right foot next to your left, and step your left foot in place, to a rhythm of "one-and-two".

The Dance

Difficulty Level: II
Choreographer: Unknown
Dance Faces: four directions
Pattern Length: 32 Beats
Suggested Music:

For practicing – "I Wanna Go Too Far" – originally recorded by Trisha Yearwood (Track 4 on your ***Free CD***).

For dancing – "Boot Scootin' Boogie" by Brooks and Dunn.

Beats	Description
	Vines
1- 4	Right vine with left scuff 1 Step **right** foot to right side 2 Step **left** foot behind **right** foot 3 Step **right** foot to right side 4 Scuff **left** foot
5- 8	Left vine with right scuff 5 Step **left** foot to left side 6 Step **right** foot behind **left** foot 7 Step **left** foot to left side 8 Scuff **right** foot
	Steps and Scuffs
9	Step **right** foot next to **left** foot
10	Scuff **left** foot
11	Step **left** foot next to **right** foot
12	Scuff **right** foot
	Twists
13	Twist right
14	Twist left
15	Twist right
16	Twist center
	Stomps and Kicks
17	Stomp-up **right** foot in place
18	Stomp-up **right** foot in place
19	Kick **right** foot forward
20-21	Right kick-ball-change 20 Kick **right** foot forward & Step ball of **right** foot next to **left** foot 21 Step **left** foot in place
22	Stomp-up **right** foot in place
23	Kick **right** foot forward
24	Kick **right** foot forward

Rock and Turn

25	Rock-step **right** foot forward
26	Hook **left** leg behind **right** leg
27	Rock-step **left** foot back
28	Chug **right** leg
29	Rock-step **right** foot back
30	Chug **left** leg
31	Step **left** foot forward
32	Scuff **right** foot and pivot on **left** foot 1/4 turn left

Repeat Pattern

Right Chug

Right Hitch

RIGHT LEG POSITIONS FOR CHUG AND HITCH

Rhythm Line:

```
secs     .....1.....2.....3.....4.....5.....6.....7.....8.....9....10
120 bpm    1  2  3  4  1  2  3  4  1  2  3  4  1  2  3  4  1  2  3  4
foot       R  L  R  L  L  R  L  R  R  L  L  R  B  B  B  B  R  R  R  R

secs     ....11....12....13....14....15....16....17....18....19....20
120 bpm  & 1  2  3  4  1  2  3  4  1  2  3  4  1  2  3  4  1  2  3  4
foot     R L  R  R  R  R  L  L  R  R  L  L  R  Repeat Pattern
```

Cues:

right / behind / right / scuff
left / behind / left / scuff
right / scuff / left / scuff
twist right / left / right / center
stomp / stomp / kick
kick-ball-change
stomp / kick / kick
rock forward / hook / back / chug
rock back / chug / forward / turn

Tennessee Twister

New Concepts, Steps and Combinations

New Concept

Wiggle Describes a body movement in which the hips and the shoulders move in opposition to one another. They are moved forward and backward in syncopated rhythm (i.e. on beats and half-beats). For example, on "one", the right shoulder moves forward and the right hip moves back; on "and", the right shoulder moves back and the right hip moves forward; on "two", the right shoulder moves forward and the right hip moves back. Wiggles may accompany steps and other body movements (for example, as you lower your body to a squat or raise your body to a standing position). The initial direction of hip and shoulder movements is not specified: do what is most comfortable for you.

The Dance

Difficulty Level: II

Choreographer: Unknown

Dance Faces: two directions

Pattern Length: 32 Beats

Suggested Music:

For practicing – "The City Put The Country Back In Me" – originally recorded by Neal McCoy (Track 2 on your ***Free CD***).

For dancing – "The South's Gonna Do It" – originally recorded by Charlie Daniels Band (Track 6 on your ***Free CD***). "Baby Likes To Rock It" by The Tractors.

Beats	Description
	Vines
1- 4	Right vine with ½ turn and left scuff
	1 Step **right** foot to right side
	2 Step **left** foot behind **right** foot
	3 Step **right** foot to right side and pivot ½ turn right
	4 Scuff **left** foot
5- 8	Left vine with right stomp
	5 Step **left** foot to left side
	6 Step **right** foot behind **left** foot
	7 Step **left** foot to left side
	8 Stomp **right** foot next to **left** foot

Heel Swivels and Wiggle

9 Swivel heels to right
10 Swivel heels to center
11 Swivel heels to left
12 Swivel heels to center

13 Swivel heels to right while wiggling down
14 Swivel heels to center while wiggling up
15 Swivel heels to left while wiggling down
16 Swivel heels to center while wiggling up

Touches

17 Touch **right** heel forward
18 Touch **right** heel forward
19 Touch **right** toe back
20 Touch **right** toe back

Right Steps** and **Slides

21 Step **right** foot forward
22 Slide **left** foot next to **right** foot
23 Step **right** foot forward
24 Slide **left** foot next to **right** foot

Forward Steps and Slides and Turns

25 Step **right** foot forward
26 Pivot on **right** foot ½ turn right (let **left** foot swing forward)
27 Step **left** foot forward
28 Slide **right** foot next to **left** foot

29 Step **left** foot forward
30 Slide **right** foot next to **left** foot
31 Step **left** foot forward
32 Pivot on **left** foot ½ turn left (let **right** foot swing forward)

Repeat Pattern

Rhythm Line:

```
secs     .....1.....2.....3.....4.....5.....6.....7.....8.....9....10
180 bpm  1 2 3 4 1 2 3 4 1 2 3 4 1 2 3 4 1 2 3 4 1 2 3 4 1 2 3 4 1 2
foot     R L R L L R L R B B B B B B B B R R R R R L R L R L L R L R
other                            w w w w
                                (wiggles)

secs     ....11....12....13....14....15....16....17....18....19....20
180 bpm  3 4 1 2 3 4 1 2 3 4 1 2 3 4 1 2 3 4 1 2 3 4 1 2 3 4 1 2 3 4
foot     L R   Repeat Pattern
other
```

Cues:

right / behind / turn / scuff
left / behind / left / stomp
heels right / center / left / center
heels right / center / left / center
heel / heel / toe / toe
right / slide / right / slide
right / turn / left / slide
left / slide / left / turn

California Coast

About this dance: This dance is a good hot weather dance – nothing moves too fast. Initially, many people have trouble with the last turn, but it is worth the practice time.

The Dance

Difficulty Level: II

Choreographer: Unknown

Dance Faces: four directions

Pattern Length: 24 Beats

Suggested Music:

For practicing – "I'm So Miserable Without You" – originally recorded by Billy Ray Cyrus (Track 7 on your ***Free CD***).

For dancing – "Fast as You" – originally recorded by Dwight Yoakam (Track 5 on your ***Free CD***). "Put Some Drive in Your Country" by Travis Tritt.

Beats	Description
	Hip Bumps
1	Step **right** foot diagonally forward and bump **right** hip diagonally forwar
2	Bump **right** hip diagonally forward
3	Bump **left** hip diagonally back
4	Bump **left** hip diagonally back
5	Step **right** foot diagonally back and bump **right** hip diagonally back
6	Bump **right** hip diagonally back
7	Bump **left** hip diagonally forward
8	Bump **left** hip diagonally forward
	Vines and Touches
9-11	Right vine
	9 Step **right** foot to right side
	10 Step **left** foot behind **right** foot
	11 Step **right** foot to right side
12	Touch **left** toe forward
13	Touch **left** toe to left side
14	Touch **left** toe back

15-17 Left vine
- 15 Step **left** foot to left side
- 16 Step **right** foot behind **left** foot
- 17 Step **left** foot to left side

Military Turns

18-19 Military turn to the left
- 18 Step **right** foot forward
- 19 Pivot on **both** feet ½ turn left

20-21 Military turn to the left
- 20 Step **right** foot forward
- 21 Pivot on **both** feet ½ turn left

22 Step **right** foot forward
23 Scuff **left** foot and pivot on **right** foot ¼ turn right
24 Step **left** foot across **right** foot

Repeat Pattern

Rhythm Line:

```
secs     .....1.....2.....3.....4.....5.....6.....7.....8.....9....10
120 bpm    1  2  3  4  1  2  3  4  1  2  3  4  1  2  3  4  1  2  3  4
foot       R  .  .  .  R  .  .  .  R  L  R  L  L  L  L  R  L  R  B  R
other      b  b  b  b  b  b  b  b
                (Hip bumps)

secs     ....11....12....13....14....15....16....17....18....19....20
120 bpm    1  2  3  4  1  2  3  4  1  2  3  4  1  2  3  4  1  2  3  4
foot       B  R  L  L  Repeat Pattern
other
```

Cues:

bump forward / forward / back / back
bump back / back / forward / forward
right / behind / right
toe forward / side / behind
left / behind / left
right / turn
right / turn
right / scuff / across

Slappin' Leather

About this dance: There are distinct regional variations of this dance in terms of the number of beats in the overall pattern. The version we present has a pattern of 36 beats. We have seen versions that have patterns of 38 and 40 beats. Why do we present this one? We tested all three using "Redneck Girl", the music to which Slappin' Leather is usually done. The 36-beat dance pattern fits best with the repetitions of melody in "Redneck Girl" (we were happy to find this, as this is also our regional version.) **Note:** make sure your hooks are high enough on beats 19, 21, and 22 so that your hands can reach your heels.

New Concepts, Steps and Combinations

New Step

Scoot Instructs you to take a small jump or hop slightly forward on the identified foot. This movement is subtle; you neither move very far nor come high off the floor.

New Combination

Heel Split Instructs you to move your heels apart and then bring them back together in two beats of music. A heel split will begin from a position in which your feet are together and your weight is supported by both feet. On beat one, move your heels apart. To execute this move, have your weight on the balls of your feet and move your right heel to the right and your left heel to the left. On beat two, move your heels back together.

The Dance

Difficulty Level: II

Choreographer: Gayle Brandon

Dance Faces: four directions

Pattern Length: 36 Beats

Suggested Music:

For practicing – "I Wanna Go Too Far" – originally recorded by Trisha Yearwood (Track 4 on your ***Free CD***).

For dancing – "Redneck Girl" – originally recorded by Bellamy Brothers (Track 11 on your ***Free CD***). "Honky Tonk Blues" by Hank Williams, Jr.

Beats	**Descriptions**
	Heel Splits
1- 2	Heel split 1 Move heels apart 2 Return heels to center
3- 4	Heel split 3 Move heels apart 4 Return heels to center
	Heel Touches
5	Touch **right** heel forward
6	Step **right** foot next to **left** foot
7	Touch **left** heel forward
8	Step **left** foot next to **right** foot
9	Touch **right** heel forward
10	Step **right** foot next to **left** foot
11	Touch **left** heel forward
12	Step **left** foot next to **right** foot
	Heel and Toe Touches
13	Touch **right** heel forward
14	Touch **right** heel forward
15	Touch **right** toe back
16	Touch **right** toe back
17	Touch **right** heel forward
18	Touch **right** toe to right side
	Boot Slaps
19	Hook **right** leg behind **left** leg and slap heel with left hand
20	Touch **right** toe to right side
21	Hook **right** leg across **left** leg and slap heel with left hand
22	Hook **right** leg to right side and slap heel with right hand and pivot on **left** foot ¼ turn left

Vines with a Hitch

23-26 Right vine with left hitch
- 23 Step **right** foot to right side
- 24 Step **left** foot behind **right** foot
- 25 Step **right** foot to right side
- 26 Hitch **left** leg

27-30 Left vine with right hitch
- 27 Step **left** foot to left side
- 28 Step **right** behind **left** foot
- 29 Step **left** foot to left side
- 30 Hitch **right** leg

Walk Back with Scoot, Step and Stomp

31 Step **right** foot back
32 Step **left** foot back
33 Step **right** foot back
34 Hitch **left** leg and scoot **right** foot forward

35 Step **left** foot forward
36 Stomp **right** foot next to **left** foot

Repeat Pattern

Variations

The basic variations involve the use of more boot slaps.

1. On count 20, instead of touching the right toe to the right side, you can hook the right leg to the right side and slap the heel with the right hand.

2. In the two vines, instead of hitching on counts 26 and 30, you can hook the "hitch" leg behind and slap its heel with the opposite hand.

3. For a really good show of balance, substitute the following for the ten steps on beats 13-22. Your right leg will be off the ground for this entire sequence (and, with luck, so will you!)
- 13 Hook **right** leg across **left** leg and slap heel with left hand
- 14 Hook **right** leg to right side and slap heel with right hand
- 15 Hook **right** leg behind **left** leg and slap heel with left hand
- 16 Hook **right** leg to right side and slap heel with right hand

- 17 Hook **right** leg across **left** leg and slap heel with left hand
- 18 Hook **right** leg to right side and slap heel with right hand
- 19 Hook **right** leg behind **left** leg and slap heel with left hand
- 20 Hook **right** leg to right side and slap heel with right hand

21-22 as before:
- 21 Hook **right** leg across **left** leg and slap heel with left hand
- 22 Hook **right** leg to right side and slap heel with right hand and pivot on **left** foot ¼ turn left

Rhythm Line:

```
secs      .....1.....2.....3.....4.....5.....6.....7.....8.....9....10
120 bpm    1  2  3  4  1  2  3  4  1  2  3  4  1  2  3  4  1  2  3  4
foot       B  B  B  B  R  R  L  L  R  R  L  L  R  R  R  R  R  R  R  R
other                                                             s
                                                             (boot slap)
```

```
secs      ....11....12....13....14....15....16....17....18....19....20
120 bpm    1  2  3  4  1  2  3  4  1  2  3  4  1  2  3  4  1  2  3  4
foot       R  R  R  L  R  L  L  R  L  R  R  L  R  R  L  R  Repeat Pattern
other      s  s
```

Cues:

split / together / split / together
right heel / together / left heel / together
right heel / together / left heel / together
heel / heel / toe / toe
heel / side
slap / side / slap / turn
right / behind / right / hitch
left / behind / left / hitch
back right / left / right / scoot
step / stomp

Ski Bumpus ("Black Velvet")

About this dance: Ski Bumpus is done in parallel or drill lines. Interestingly, when the same steps are done in contra lines, the dance is called Black Velvet or White Horse. Dance descriptions for the contra versions usually begin with the toe touches (beat 21, here) but the sequence of steps is the same.

New Concepts, Steps and Combinations

New Combination

Jazz Box Instructs you to make three steps, in a specified order, to three beats of music. A jazz box will be described as either right or left, based on the foot that makes the crossing move and leads the jazz box. On beat one, the leading foot steps across the following foot. On beat two, the following foot steps back. On beat three, the leading foot steps to the side (parallel to and shoulder width away from the following foot). Note that you will touch three corners of an imaginary square (or box) as you make these three steps.

As with vines, a fourth, "finishing move" is often specified for the foot that is free to move after the jazz box (and, actually, may complete the box). In some dances, rather than having a "finishing move", the jazz box is preceded by a step (to make up 4 steps). Some jazz box instructions may include turns (giving a funny look to the imaginary box). Consequently, you will see directions like "right jazz box with left step" or "right step with left jazz box" or "right jazz box with ¼ turn right".

For example, "right jazz box with left step" instructs you to: step your right foot across your left foot, step your left foot back, step your right foot to the right side, and, finally, step your left foot next to your right foot, to a rhythm of 1, 2, 3, 4.

The Dance

Difficulty Level: II

Choreographer: Linda DeFord

Dance Faces: one direction

Pattern Length: 40 Beats

Suggested Music:

For practicing – "I'm So Miserable Without You" – originally recorded by Billy Ray Cyrus (Track 7 on your ***Free CD***).

For dancing – "Walkin' Away A Winner" – originally by Kathy Mattea (Track 1 on your ***Free CD***). "Men" by Forrester Sisters. "Never Giving Up on Love" by Michael Martin Murphy.

Beats	**Description**	
	Shuffles and Turns	
1- 2	Right shuffle forward	
	1	Step **right** foot forward
	&	Step **left** foot next to **right** foot
	2	Step **right** foot forward
3- 4	Left shuffle forward	
	3	Step **left** foot forward
	&	Step **right** foot next to **left** foot
	4	Step **left** foot forward
5- 6	Military turn to the left	
	5	Step **right** foot forward
	6	Pivot on **both** feet ½ turn left
7- 8	Right shuffle forward	
	7	Step **right** foot forward
	&	Step **left** foot next to **right** foot
	8	Step **right** foot forward
9-10	Left shuffle forward	
	9	Step **left** foot forward
	&	Step **right** foot next to **left** foot
	10	Step **left** foot forward
11-12	Military turn to the left	
	11	Step **right** foot forward
	12	Pivot on **both** feet ½ turn left
	Jazz Boxes	
13-16	Right jazz box with left step	
	13	Step **right** foot across **left** foot
	14	Step **left** foot back
	15	Step **right** foot to right side
	16	Step **left** foot next to **right** foot

17-20 Right jazz box with left step
- 17 Step **right** foot across **left** foot
- 18 Step **left** foot back
- 19 Step **right** foot to right side
- 20 Step **left** foot next to **right** foot

Toe Touches

21 Touch **right** toe to right side
22 Step **right** foot next to **left** foot
23 Touch **left** toe to left side
24 Step **left** foot next to **right** foot

25 Touch **right** toe to right side
26 Step **right** foot next to **left** foot
27 Touch **left** toe to left side
28 Step **left** foot next to **right** foot

Kick-Ball-Changes and Turns

29-30 Right kick-ball-change
- 29 Kick **right** foot forward
- & Step ball of **right** foot next to **left** foot
- 30 Step **left** foot in place

31-32 Right kick-ball-change
- 31 Kick **right** foot forward
- & Step ball of **right** foot next to **left** foot
- 32 Step **left** foot in place

33-34 Military turn to the left
- 33 Step **right** foot forward
- 34 Pivot on **both** feet 1/2 turn left

35-36 Right kick-ball-change
- 35 Kick **right** foot forward
- & Step ball of **right** foot next to **left** foot
- 36 Step **left** foot in place

37-38 Right kick-ball-change
- 37 Kick **right** foot forward
- & Step ball of **right** foot next to **left** foot
- 38 Step **left** foot in place

39-40 Military turn to the left
- 39 Step **right** foot forward
- 40 Pivot on **both** feet 1/2 turn left

Repeat Pattern

Rhythm Line:

```
secs      .....1.....2.....3.....4.....5.....6.....7.....8.....9....10
90 bpm       1 & 2   3 & 4   1   2   3 & 4   1 & 2   3   4   1   2   3
foot         R L R   L R L   R   B   R L R   L R L   R   B   R   L   R

secs      ....11....12....13....14....15....16....17....18....19....20
90 bpm       4   1   2   3   4   1   2   3   4   1   2   3   4   1 & 2
foot         L   R   L   R   L   R   R   L   L   R   R   L   L   R R L

secs      ....21....22....23....24....25....26....27....28....29....30
90 bpm       3 & 4   1   2   3 & 4   1 & 2   3   4   1 & 2  3 & 4  1  2
foot         R R L   R   B   R R L   R R L   R   B   Repeat Pattern
```

Cues:

right - together - right / left - together - left
step / turn
right - together - right / left - together - left
step / turn
cross / back / side / together
cross / back / side / together
right / together / left / together
right / together / left / together
kick - ball - change / kick - ball - change
step / turn
kick - ball - change / kick - ball - change
step / turn

Personality

About this dance: We wish we knew the choreographer for this dance so that we could resolve some controversy on how the dance steps relate to the beats of music. Everyone we have seen do this dance has done the same footwork, but the written dance descriptions do not always agree: some of them indicate that there are no holds after the weaves; some describe the weaves and heel touches in double time ("quick" heel touches and syncopated two-count weaves); and some descriptions leave the count in doubt. We believe that the holds and slow heel touches capture the Personality that we see.

New Concepts, Steps and Combinations

New Concept

Slow Instructs you to perform the designated step over two beats of music rather than one. For example, "slow touch **right** heel forward" instructs you to use two beats of music to touch your right heel to the floor. Initially, the slow move may feel clumsy and seem difficult to do. It may help to think about a slow heel touch as a chug on beat one and a heel touch on beat two.

Most steps are choreographed to match one beat of music. Although not used in this book, a step done to one beat of music is often called a "quick" step. It is in contrast to the name "quick" that steps done to two beats of music are called "slow". Steps done on half-beats of music are often called "syncopated".

Almost any step can be lengthened to make it a slow step. Slow *jumps*, however, are only done by Michael Jordan.

New Combination

Toe Strut Instructs you to execute two movements of one foot in two beats of music. The strutting foot, and the direction of the strut (i.e. forward or backward) will be specified in the dance description. On beat one, the toe is touched in the direction of travel. On beat two, the heel is lowered and weight is transferred to that foot.

For example, "left toe strut forward" instructs you, on beat one, to touch your left toe forward. On beat two, lower your left heel to the floor and step down on your left foot.

Weave Instructs you to make a series of movements in which steps across and behind alternate with steps to the side. The first step in a weave will always be across or behind. The number of beats involved in the weave will be specified in the dance description and each step will be done to one beat of music. The direction of the weave (for example, “to left” or “diagonally right”) and whether the first move is across or behind will be specified in the dance description. Note: because weaves begin with the first foot to move stepping across or behind, the first foot to move is the foot opposite the direction of the weave.

For example, “beats 1-4 Weave to right (begin across)” tells you to: on one, step your left foot across your right; on two, step your right foot to the right side; on three, step your left foot behind your right; and on four, again step your right foot to the right side.

Doing a weave may feel very much like doing a vine. In fact, a weave is a special type of vine. It is different from the vines you have danced so far in that it begins with a crossing step, and the crossing steps are alternately in front of and behind the weighted foot.

The "Slow-Jump"

The Dance

Difficulty Level: II

Choreographer: Unknown

Dance Faces: one direction

Pattern Length: 64 Beats

Suggested music:

For practicing – "Walkin' Away A Winner" – originally recorded by Kathy Mattea (Track 1 on your ***Free CD***).

For dancing – "Walkin' Away A Winner" – originally recorded by Kathy Mattea (Track 1 on your ***Free CD***). "Texas Tattoo" by Gibson-Miller Band.

Beats	Description
	Toe Struts Forward
1- 2	Right toe strut forward 1 Touch **right** toe forward 2 Lower **right** heel (step **right** foot down)
3- 4	Left toe strut forward 3 Touch **left** toe forward 4 Lower **left** heel (step **left** foot down)
5- 6	Right toe strut forward 5 Touch **right** toe forward 6 Lower **right** heel (step **right** foot down)
7- 8	Left toe strut forward 7 Touch **left** toe forward 8 Lower **left** heel (step **left** foot down)
	Slides to Side
9	Step **right** foot to right side
10	Slide **left** foot next to **right** foot
11	Step **right** foot to right side
12	Slide-up **left** foot next to **right** foot
13	Step **left** foot to left side
14	Slide **right** foot next to **left** foot
15	Step **left** foot to left side
16	Slide-up **right** foot next to **left** foot
	Toe Struts Back
17-18	Right toe strut back 17 Touch **right** toe back 18 Lower **right** heel (step **right** foot down)
19-20	Left toe strut back 19 Touch **left** toe back 20 Lower **left** heel (step **left** foot down)

21-22 Right toe strut back
- 21 Touch **right** toe back
- 22 Lower **right** heel (step **right** foot down)

23-24 Left toe strut back
- 23 Touch **left** toe back
- 24 Lower **left** heel (step **left** foot down)

Slides to Side

25 Step **right** foot to right side
26 Slide **left** foot next to **right** foot
27 Step **right** foot to right side
28 Slide-up **left** foot next to **right** foot

29 Step **left** foot to left side
30 Slide **right** foot next to **left** foot
31 Step **left** foot to left side
32 Slide-up **right** foot next to **left** foot

Heels and Weaves

33-34 Slow touch **right** heel diagonally forward
35-36 Slow touch **right** heel diagonally forward

37-39 Weave to left (begin behind)
- 37 Step **right** foot behind **left** foot
- 38 Step **left** foot to left side
- 39 Step **right** foot across **left** foot

40 Hold

41-42 Slow touch **left** heel diagonally forward
43-44 Slow touch **left** heel diagonally forward

45-47 Weave to right (begin behind)
- 45 Step **left** foot behind **right** foot
- 46 Step **right** foot to right side
- 47 Step **left** foot across **right** foot
- 48 Hold

49-50 Slow touch **right** heel diagonally forward
51-52 Slow touch **right** heel diagonally forward

53-55 Weave to left (begin behind)
- 53 Step **right** foot behind **left** foot
- 54 Step **left** foot to left side
- 55 Step **right** foot across **left** foot

56 Hold

57-58 Slow touch **left** heel diagonally forward
59-60 Slow touch **left** heel diagonally forward

61-63 Weave to right (begin behind)
- 61 Step **left** foot behind **right** foot
- 62 Step **right** foot to right side
- 63 Step **left** foot across **right** foot

64 Hold

Repeat Pattern

Variation

To dance Personality as a four wall dance, we have seen the following suggested: on the right step-slides done on beats 25-28, make a ¼ turn to the right on beat 27.

25 Step **right** foot to right side
26 Slide **left** foot next to **right** foot
27 Step **right** foot to right side and pivot ¼ turn right
28 Touch **left** foot next to **right** foot

Rhythm Line:

```
secs     .....1.....2.....3.....4.....5.....6.....7.....8.....9....10
120 bpm    1  2  3  4  1  2  3  4  1  2  3  4  1  2  3  4  1  2  3  4
foot       R  R  L  L  R  R  L  L  R  L  R  L  L  R  L  R  R  R  L  L

secs     ....11....12....13....14....15....16....17....18....19....20
120 bpm    1  2  3  4  1  2  3  4  1  2  3  4  1  2  3  4  1  2  3  4
foot       R  R  L  L  R  L  R  L  L  R  L  R  (-R- )(-R- )R  L  R  .
                                                slow  slow

secs     ....21....22....23....24....25....26....27....28....29....30
120 bpm    1  2  3  4  1  2  3  4  1  2  3  4  1  2  3  4  1  2  3  4
foot     (-L- )(-L- )  L  R  L  .  (-R- )(-R- )R  L  R  .  (-L- )(-L- )
          slow  slow               slow  slow              slow  slow

secs     ....31....32....33....34....35....36....37....38....39....40
120 bpm    1  2  3  4  1  2  3  4  1  2  3  4  1  2  3  4  1  2  3  4
foot       L  R  L  .  Repeat Pattern
```

Cues:

toe / heel / toe / heel
toe / heel / toe / heel
right / slide / right / touch
left / slide / left / touch
toe / heel / toe / heel
toe / heel / toe / heel
right / slide / right / touch
left / slide / left / touch
slow / heel / slow / heel
behind / step / across / hold
slow / heel / slow / heel
behind / step / across / hold
slow / heel / slow / heel
behind / step / across / hold
slow / heel / slow / heel
behind / step / across / hold

Alabama Driver

About this dance: Alabama Driver is a short, but tricky dance for the beginner. It involves several cross steps and weight changes.

The Dance

Difficulty Level: II

Choreographer: Unknown

Dance Faces: four directions

Pattern Length: 18 Beats

Suggested Music:

For practicing – "Wher'm I Gonna Live When I Get Home" – originally recorded by Billy Ray Cyrus (Track 9 on your ***Free CD***).

For dancing – "Fast as You" – originally recorded by Dwight Yoakam (Track 5 on your ***Free CD***). "Rock My World" by Brooks and Dunn

Beats	Description
	Touches
1	Touch **right** toe to right side
2	Touch **right** toe next to **left** foot
3	Touch **right** toe to right side
4	Step **right** foot next to **left** foot
5	Touch **left** toe to left side
6	Touch **left** toe next to **right** foot
7	Touch **left** toe to left side
8	Step **left** foot next to **right** foot
9	Touch **right** heel forward
10	Touch **right** toe back
	Steps and Scuffs
11	Step **right** foot forward
12	Scuff **left** foot and pivot on **right** foot 1/4 turn right
13	Step **left** foot across **right** foot
14	Scuff **right** foot
	Jazz Box
15-18	Right jazz box with left across
	15 Step **right** foot across **left** foot
	16 Step **left** foot back
	17 Step **right** foot to right side
	18 Step **left** foot across **right** foot

Repeat Pattern

Rhythm Line:

```
secs      .....1.....2.....3.....4.....5.....6.....7.....8.....9....10
180 bpm   1 2 3 4 1 2 3 4 1 2 3 4 1 2 3 4 1 2 3 4 1 2 3 4 1 2 3 4 1 2
foot      R R R R L L L L R R R L L R R L R L Repeat Pattern
```

Cues:

toe / together / toe / together
toe / together / toe / together
heel / toe
right / scuff / across / scuff
across / back / right / across

Cows line dancing – it's udderly ridiculous!

Level III

Hooked On Country

About this dance: This dance has an unusual background. It was choreographed, apparently, not to accompany a single popular country song, but to accompany a medley of country songs performed by the Atlanta Pops Orchestra. Dancing "Hooked on Country" to that medley always feels like a "whole body" salute to Country and Western music.

Most Country and Western dances begin on the same beat as the lyrics. "Hooked on Country" by the Atlanta Pops Orchestra has no lyrics and a long, slow introductory passage ("Tennessee Waltz"). When do you begin? The slow tempo will change to a noticeably more rapid tempo and you start on the 13th beat after this change in tempo.

The Dance

Difficulty Level: III

Choreographer: Unknown

Dance Faces: four directions

Pattern Length: 32 beats

Suggested Music:

For practicing – "Walkin' Away a Winner" – originally recorded by Kathy Mattea (Track 1 on your ***Free CD***).

For dancing – "Redneck Girl" – originally recorded by Bellamy Brothers (Track 11 on your ***Free CD***). "(Just) Hooked on Country" by Atlanta Pops Orchestra. "Walk On" by Reba McEntire

---

Beats	Description
	Shuffles Back and Walk Forward
1-2	Right shuffle back
	1 Step **right** foot back
	& Step **left** foot next to **right** foot
	2 Step **right** foot back
3- 4	Left shuffle back
	3 Step **left** foot back
	& Step **right** foot next to **left** foot
	4 Step **left** foot back
5	Step **right** foot forward
6	Step **left** foot forward

7 Step **right** foot forward
8 Kick **left** foot forward and clap

Walk Back with Cross Step

9 Step **left** foot back
10 Step **right** foot back

11 Step **left** foot back
& Step **right** foot back
12 Step **left** foot across **right** foot

Vines with Kicks and Claps

13-16 Right vine with left kick and clap
 13 Step **right** foot to right side
 14 Step **left** foot behind **right** foot
 15 Step **right** foot to right side
 16 Kick **left** foot across **right** leg and clap

17-20 Left vine with right kick and clap
 17 Step **left** foot to left side
 18 Step **right** foot behind **left** foot
 19 Step **left** foot to left side
 20 Kick **right** foot across **left** leg and clap

Steps and Kicks

21 Step **right** foot next to **left** foot
22 Kick **left** foot across **right** leg and clap
23 Step **left** foot next to **right** foot
24 Kick **right** foot across **left** leg and clap

Touches and Turn

25 Touch **right** heel forward
26 Touch **right** heel forward
27 Touch **right** toe back
28 Touch **right** toe back

29 Step **right** foot forward
30 Pivot on **both** feet 1/4 turn left
31 Stomp-up **right** foot next to **left** foot
32 Kick **right** foot forward

Repeat Pattern

Variation

For extra turning, you can substitute two military turns to the left on beats 25-28:
25-26 Military turn to the left
 25 Step **right** foot forward
 26 Pivot on **both** feet 1/2 turn left

27-28 Military turn to the left
 27 Step **right** foot forward
 28 Pivot on **both** feet 1/2 turn left

Rhythm Line:

secs	1	2		3		4		5	6		7		8		9		10
120 bpm	1 & 2	3 & 4	1	2	3	4	1	2	3 & 4	1	2	3	4	1	2	3	4
foot	R L R	L R L	R	L	R	L	L	R	L R L	R	L	R	L	L	R	L	R
other						c (clap)							c				c

secs		11		12		13		14		15		16	17	18		19		20
120 bpm	1	2	3	4	1	2	3	4	1	2	3	4	1 & 2	3 & 4	1	2	3	4
foot	R	L	L	R	R	R	R	R	R	B	R	R	*Repeat Pattern*					
other		c		c														

Cues:

back – together – right / back – together – left
right / left / right / kick
back / back / left – right – cross
right / behind / right / kick
left / behind / left / kick
right / kick / left / kick
heel / heel / toe / toe
step / turn / stomp / kick

Tush Push

About this dance: This is one of the most frequently danced line dances. It was introduced about 1981 and its popularity does not appear to be waning. It is done in either drill lines, as the other line dances in this section, or in spoke-lines, as the dances in the "circle" section.

The movement on beats 5, 9, 10 and 11 of this pattern will take some practice as it involves a weight change so quick that it often looks like a jump.

New Concepts, Steps and Combinations

New Combination

Hip Roll Instructs you to move your hips around in a specified number of beats. The direction (clockwise or counter-clockwise), extent of rotation (half-circle or full circle), and the starting position of the hips (e.g. left diagonal back) will be specified in the dance description. The hip roll is a continuous movement over the specified beats of music. The hips begin a hip roll by moving out from under the body in the direction specified and remain out from under the body until they reach the roll's end position. As with a hip bump, hip rolls are generally easier to execute if the weight is supported by both feet and the knees are bent slightly. Unlike the hip bump, which is completed in a single beat of music, the hip roll will take several beats of music to complete.

For example, "beats 1-4 Full hip roll, counter-clockwise (begin left hip diagonally back)" instructs you to move your hips to the left diagonal back position (if they are not already there), push them to the right, then diagonally forward, and next, keeping the hips pushed out, circle them left and back until they reach their starting position.

The Dance

Difficulty Level: III **Choreographer:** Jim and Martie Ferrazzanno

Dance Faces: four directions **Pattern Length**: 40 Beats

Suggested Music:

For practicing – "Wher'm I Gonna Live When I Get Home" – originally recorded by Billy Ray Cyrus (Track 9 on your ***Free CD***).

For dancing – "Fast as You" – originally recorded by Dwight Yoakam (Track 5 on your ***Free CD***). "Romeo" by Dolly Parton.

Beats	Description
	Touches
1	Touch **right** heel diagonally forward
2	Touch **right** heel diagonally forward
3	Touch **right** heel diagonally forward
4	Touch **right** heel diagonally forward
5	Step **right** foot home and touch **left** heel diagonally forward
6	Touch **left** heel diagonally forward
7	Touch **left** heel diagonally forward
8	Touch **left** heel diagonally forward
9	Step **left** foot home and touch **right** heel diagonally forward
10	Step **right** foot home and touch **left** heel diagonally forward
11	Step **left** foot home and touch **right** heel diagonally forward
12	Clap (**right** foot remains diagonally forward from beat 11)
	Hip Bumps and Hip Rolls
13	Lower **right** toe (step **right** foot down) and bump **right** hip diagonally forward
14	Bump **right** hip diagonally forward
15	Bump **left** hip diagonally back
16	Bump **left** hip diagonally back
17-18	Half hip roll, clockwise (begin right hip diagonally forward)
19-20	Half hip roll, clockwise (begin right hip diagonally forward)
	Shuffles and Rocks
21-22	Right shuffle forward
	21 Step **right** foot forward
	& Step **left** foot next to **right** foot
	22 Step **right** foot forward
23	Rock-step **left** foot forward
24	Rock back on **right** foot

25-26 Left shuffle back
- 25 Step **left** foot back
- & Step **right** foot next to **left** foot
- 26 Step **left** foot back

- 27 Rock-step **right** foot back
- 28 Rock forward on **left** foot

Shuffles and Turns

29-30 Right shuffle forward
- 29 Step **right** foot forward
- & Step **left** foot next to **right** foot
- 30 Step **right** foot forward

31-32 Military turn to the right
- 31 Step **left** foot forward
- 32 Pivot on **both** feet ½ turn right

33-34 Left shuffle forward
- 33 Step **left** foot forward
- & Step **right** foot next to **left** foot
- 34 Step **left** foot forward

35-36 Military turn to the left
- 35 Step **right** foot forward
- 36 Pivot on **both** feet ½ turn left

Turn and Clap

37 Step **right** foot forward
38 Pivot on **both** feet ¼ turn left
39 Stomp **right** foot next to **left** foot
40 Clap

Repeat Pattern

Variations

1. To avoid the quick weight change on beat 5, many dancers do the following:

1 Touch **right** heel diagonally forward
2 Touch **right** toe next to **left** foot
3 Touch **right** heel diagonally forward
4 Step **right** foot next to **left** foot

5 Touch **left** heel diagonally forward
6 Touch **left** toe next to **right** foot
7 Touch **left** heel diagonally forward
8 Step **left** foot next to **right** foot

2. To avoid the quick weight changes on beats 9, 10 and 11, many dancers replace those beats of the pattern with the following:

9 Twist right
10 Twist left
11 Twist center
12 Step **right** foot diagonally forward and clap.

3. Some dance descriptions replace the two half-circle hip rolls at beats 17 to 20 with four hip bumps: right diagonally forward, left diagonally back, right diagonally forward, and left diagonally back.

Rhythm Line:

```
secs       .....1.....2.....3.....4.....5.....6.....7.....8.....9....10
120 bpm      1   2   3   4   1   2   3   4   1   2   3   4   1   2   3   4   1   2   3   4
foot         R   R   R   R   B   L   L   L   B   B   B   .   .   .   .   .   .   .   .   .
other                                                    c   b   b   b   b   (-h-)   (-h-)
                                                     (clap)   (bumps)     (hip rolls)

secs       ....11....12....13....14....15....16....17....18....19....20
120 bpm      1 & 2   3   4   1 & 2   3   4   1 & 2   3   4   1 & 2   3   4   1   2   3   4
foot         R L R   L   R   L R L   R   L   R L R   L   B   L R L   R   B   R   B   R   .
other                                                                                    c
                                                                                      (clap)
```

Cues:

heel / heel / heel / heel
heel / heel / heel / heel
right / left / right / clap
bump / bump / bump / bump
roll / roll / roll / roll
right-together-right / rock forward / back
back-together-back / rock back / forward
right-together-right / step / turn
left-together-left / step / turn
step / turn / stomp / clap

Go-Go's Stomp

About this dance: Dances are named for different reasons. This one is named after the nickname of one of the choreographers. However, you may often hear people call this dance, the Go-Go Stomp (named after the short, white boots of the sixties?).

New Concepts, Steps and Combinations

New Combinations

Heel Twist Instructs you to make two movements in two beats of music. The foot which moves will be identified in the dance description. On beat one, the heel touches forward with foot turned in. On beat two, the toe swivels so that it moves from pointing inside to pointing forward and weight is placed on the foot (i.e. the foot steps down). Note: a heel twist is like a heel strut except that on beat one in a heel twist, the toes point up and inward, but in a heel strut the toes point up.

For example, "right heel twist" instructs you, on one, to touch your right heel forward with foot turned in, and on two, keeping your heel touched to the floor, to swivel your right foot (so the toe points forward) and step down on your right foot.

The Dance

Difficulty Level: III **Choreographer:** Gloria (Go-Go) and Emmitt Nelson

Dance Faces: one direction **Pattern Length**: 68 Beats

Suggested Music:

For practicing – "Talk Some" – originally recorded by Billy Ray Cyrus (Track 3 on your ***Free CD***).

For dancing – "Any Man of Mine" by Shania Twain. "Third Rock From The Sun" by Joe Diffie. "Baby Likes to Rock It" by The Tractors.

Beats	Description
	Heel Twists and Stomps
1- 2	Right heel twist
	1 Touch **right** heel (*foot turned in*) forward
	2 Swivel **right** toe to center (step **right** foot down)
3	Stomp **left** foot next to **right** foot
4	Hold

5- 6 Right heel twist
 5 Touch **right** heel (*foot turned in*) forward
 6 Swivel **right** toe to center (step **right** foot down)
7 Stomp **left** foot next to **right** foot
8 Hold

9-10 Right heel twist
 9 Touch **right** heel (*foot turned in*) forward
 10 Swivel **right** toe to center (step **right** foot down)
11 Stomp **left** foot next to **right** foot
12 Hold

13-14 Right heel twist
 13 Touch **right** heel (*foot turned in*) forward
 14 Swivel **right** toe to center (step **right** foot down)
15 Stomp **left** foot next to **right** foot
16 Hold

Rock and Turn

17 Rock-step **right** foot forward
18 Rock back on **left** foot
19 Rock-step **right** foot back
20 Rock forward on **left** foot

21 Step **right** foot forward
22 Pivot on **both** feet 1/4 turn left
23 Step **right** foot forward
24 Pivot on **both** feet 1/4 turn left

Heel Twists and Stomps

25-26 Right heel twist
 25 Touch **right** heel (*foot turned in*) forward
 26 Swivel **right** toe to center (step **right** foot down)
27 Stomp **left** foot next to **right** foot
28 Hold

29-30 Right heel twist
 29 Touch **right** heel (*foot turned in*) forward
 30 Swivel **right** toe to center (step **right** foot down)
31 Stomp **left** foot next to **right** foot
32 Hold

33-34 Right heel twist
 33 Touch **right** heel (*foot turned in*) forward
 34 Swivel **right** toe to center (step **right** foot down)
35 Stomp **left** foot next to **right** foot
36 Hold

37-38 Right heel twist
 37 Touch **right** heel (*foot turned in*) forward
 38 Swivel **right** toe to center (step **right** foot down)
39 Stomp **left** foot next to **right** foot
40 Hold

Side Steps and Slides

41	Step **right** foot to right side
42	Touch **left** foot next to **right** foot
43	Step **left** foot to left side
44	Touch **right** foot next to **left** foot
45	Step **right** foot to right side
46	Slide **left** foot next to **right** foot
47	Step **right** foot to right side
48	Touch **left** foot next to **right** foot
49	Step **left** foot to left side
50	Touch **right** foot next to **left** foot
51	Step **right** foot to right side
52	Touch **left** foot next to **right** foot
53	Step **left** foot to left side
54	Slide **right** foot next to **left** foot
55	Step **left** foot to left side
56	Touch **right** foot next to **left** foot
57	Step **right** foot forward and pivot 1/4 turn left
58	Touch **left** foot next to **right** foot
59	Step **left** foot to left side
60	Touch **right** foot next to **left** foot
61	Step **right** foot forward and pivot1/4 turn left
62	Touch **left** foot next to **right** foot
63	Step **left** foot to left side
64	Touch **right** foot next to **left** foot

Heel Struts

65-66 Right heel strut

- 65 Touch **right** heel forward
- 66 Lower **right** toe (step **right** foot down)

67-68 Left heel strut

- 67 Touch **left** heel forward
- 68 Lower **left** toe (step **left** foot down)

Repeat Pattern

Rhythm Line:

```
secs      .....1.....2.....3.....4.....5.....6.....7.....8.....9....10
120 bpm     1  2  3  4  1  2  3  4  1  2  3  4  1  2  3  4  1  2  3  4
foot        R  R  L  .  R  R  L  .  R  R  L  .  R  R  L  .  R  L  R  L

secs      ....11....12....13....14....15....16....17....18....19....20
120 bpm     1  2  3  4  1  2  3  4  1  2  3  4  1  2  3  4  1  2  3  4
foot        R  B  R  B  R  R  L  .  R  R  L  .  R  R  L  .  R  R  L  .

secs      ....21....22....23....24....25....26....27....28....29....30
120 bpm     1  2  3  4  1  2  3  4  1  2  3  4  1  2  3  4  1  2  3  4
foot        R  L  L  R  R  L  R  L  L  R  R  L  L  R  L  R  R  L  L  R

secs      ....31....32....33....34....35....36....37....38....39....40
120 bpm     1  2  3  4  1  2  3  4  1  2  3  4  1  2  3  4  1  2  3  4
foot        R  L  L  R  R  R  L  L  Repeat Pattern
```

Cues:

heel / twist / stomp / hold
heel / twist / stomp / hold
heel / twist / stomp / hold
heel / twist / stomp / hold
rock forward / back / back / forward
right / turn / right / turn
heel / twist / stomp / hold
heel / twist / stomp / hold
heel / twist / stomp / hold
heel / twist / stomp / hold
right / touch / left / touch
right / slide / right / touch
left / touch / right / touch
left / slide / left / touch
turn / touch / side / touch
turn / touch / side / touch
heel / toe / heel / toe

Thunderfoot

About this dance: This dance is an opportunity to let the cowboy in you be heard. Danced most often to "Copperhead Road" by Steve Earle, dancers often shout "yippee" and "yah-yah" to cues from a disc-jockey or dance leader.

The side step-slides in this dance are done with the entire body facing diagonally in the direction of travel. This style gives the dance a twisting look as the double step-slides give way to single step-slides and the latter are followed by pivot turns (beats 21 and 22). Note that the pivots are quick, twisting movements. On the second, you pivot 180 degrees in one beat of music. This last pivot must bring you to a position in which you are ¼ turn left from where you started the pattern!

New Concepts, Steps and Combinations

New Concept

Face Instructs you to change, temporarily, the orientation of your body. Face is used with foot directions to add body styling, but it does not change your reference point or wall. "Face" is different from "turn" in that "face" directs body orientation only for the beat(s) on which it appears, however, "turn" results in a permanent change of body orientation and a new reference point or wall.

Touch Right Heel Forward

Hook Right Leg Across Left Leg

Touch Right Heel Forward

Step Right Foot Next To Left Foot

RIGHT BOOT HOOK COMBINATION

The Dance

Difficulty Level: III

Choreographer: Unknown

Dance Faces: four directions

Pattern Length: 36 Beats

Suggested Music:

For practicing – "I Wanna Go Too Far" – originally recorded by Trisha Yearwood (Track 4 on your ***Free CD***).

For dancing – "Redneck Girl" – originally recorded by Bellamy Brothers (Track 11 on your ***Free CD***). "Copperhead Road" by Steve Earle.

Beats	Description
	Boot Hooks
1- 4	Right boot hook combination
	1 Touch **right** heel *(foot turned out)* diagonally forward
	2 Hook **right** leg *(foot turned out)* in front of **left** leg
	3 Touch **right** heel *(foot turned out)* diagonally forward
	4 Step **right** foot next to **left** foot
5- 8	Left boot hook combination
	5 Touch **left** heel *(foot turned out)* diagonally forward
	6 Hook **left** leg *(foot turned out)* in front of **right** leg
	7 Touch **left** heel *(foot turned out)* diagonally forward
	8 Step **left** foot next to **right** foot
	Two Step-Slides Right
	(on the next 3 beats face diagonally right)
9	Step **right** foot to right side
10	Slide **left** foot next to **right** foot
11	Step **right** foot to right side
12	Slide-up **left** foot next to **right** foot, face forward
	Two Step-Slides Left
	(on the next 3 beats face diagonally left)
13	Step **left** foot to left side
14	Slide **right** foot next to **left** foot
15	Step **left** foot to left side
16	Slide-up **right** foot next to **left** foot, face forward
	One Step-Slide Right
17	Step **right** foot to right, face diagonally right
18	Slide-up **left** foot next to **right** foot, face forward
	One Step-Slide Left
19	Step **left** foot to left, face diagonally left
20	Slide-up **right** foot next to **left** foot, face forward

Pivots and Kicks

21 Pivot on **both** feet 1/4 turn right
22 Pivot on **both** feet 1/2 turn left
23 Kick **right** foot forward
24 Kick **right** foot forward

Walk Back and Scoot Forward

25 Step **right** foot back
26 Step **left** foot back
27 Touch **right** toe back
28 Step **right** foot forward

29 Hitch **left** leg and scoot **right** foot forward
30 Step **left** foot forward
31 Hitch **right** leg and scoot **left** foot forward
32 Stomp **right** foot next to **left** foot

Heel Swivels

33 Swivel heels to left
34 Swivel heels to center
35 Swivel heels to right
36 Swivel heels to center

Repeat Pattern

Rhythm Line:

```
secs     .....1.....2.....3.....4.....5.....6.....7.....8.....9....10
120 bpm    1  2  3  4  1  2  3  4  1  2  3  4  1  2  3  4  1  2  3  4
foot       R  R  R  R  L  L  L  L  R  L  R  L  L  R  L  R  R  L  L  R

secs     ....11....12....13....14....15....16....17....18....19....20
120 bpm    1  2  3  4  1  2  3  4  1  2  3  4  1  2  3  4  1  2  3  4
foot       B  B  R  R  R  L  R  R  R  L  L  R  B  B  B  B  Repeat Pattern
```

Cues:

heel / hook / heel / home
heel / hook / heel / home
right / slide / right / slide
left / slide / left / slide
right / slide / left / slide
twist / twist / kick / kick
back / back / touch / forward
scoot / left / scoot / stomp
left / center / right / center

Reggae Cowboy II

About this dance: Reggae Cowboy II has also been called Bayou Bangle. The different names certainly reflect different rhythms and cultures. The Caribbean may seem to be an unlikely locale for Country and Western music, but on some of the islands, Country and Western is really big. While visiting Barbados, we noticed a mix of Country and Western and Caribbean music and clothing. So, why not a Reggae cowboy dance? Our dance description brings out the "Reggae" feel on beats 1-8. Some dance descriptions substitute 4 shuffles with a clap on each step (12 claps!) which, we believe, detracts from the feel of the Islands but does fit a Bayou mood.

New Concepts, Steps and Combinations

New Combination

Three-Step Turn

Instructs you to make one full turn in three steps to three beats of music. The turn will be labelled right or left, indicating the direction of the turn and the foot that leads the combination. On one, step your lead foot to the side and pivot 1/2 turn in the indicated direction. On two, step your following foot to the side and pivot another 1/2 turn in the indicated direction. On three, step your lead foot to the side.

For example, a "three-step turn to left" means: on beat one, step your left foot to your left side and pivot 1/2 turn left; on beat two, step your right foot to your right side and pivot 1/2 turn to the left; on beat three, step your left foot to your left.

Although we do not use this label, three-step turns are sometimes called "rolling vines". Three-step turns are often done as variations in place of vines or step-slide-step patterns. When three-step turns are used in 4/4 time music, a fourth finishing move is often specified with the turn.

The Dance

Difficulty Level: III

Choreographer: Unknown

Dance Faces: four directions

Pattern Length: 48 Beats

Suggested Music:

For practicing – "I'm So Miserable Without You" – originally recorded by Billy Ray Cyrus (Track 7 on your ***Free CD***).

For dancing – "Shut Up And Kiss Me" – originally recorded by Mary Chapin Carpenter (Track 8 on your ***Free CD***). "Reggae Cowboy" by Bellamy Brothers.

Beats	Description
	Walk Forward with Claps
1	Step **right** foot forward
&	Clap
2	Clap
3	Step **left** foot forward
&	Clap
4	Clap
5	Step **right** foot forward
&	Clap
6	Clap
7	Step **left** foot forward
&	Clap
8	Clap
	Walk Back with a Hitch
9	Step **right** foot back
10	Step **left** foot back
11	Step **right** foot back
12	Hitch **left** leg
13	Step **left** foot back
14	Step **right** foot back
15	Step **left** foot back
16	Hitch **right** leg
	Latin Step-Slides
17	Latin-step **right** foot to right side
18	Latin-slide **left** foot next to **right** foot
19	Latin-step **right** foot to right side
20	Latin-slide-up **left** foot next to **right** foot

21	Latin-step **left** foot to left side
22	Latin-slide **right** foot next to **left** foot
23	Latin-step **left** foot to left side
24	Latin-slide-up **right** foot next to **left** foot
25	Latin-step **right** foot to right side
26	Latin-slide **left** foot next to **right** foot
27	Latin-step **right** foot to right side
28	Latin-slide-up **left** foot next to **right** foot
29	Latin-step **left** foot to left side
30	Latin-slide **right** foot next to **left** foot
31	Latin-step **left** foot to left side
32	Latin-slide-up **right** foot next to **left** foot

Shuffles Around The Bases
(see diagram below)

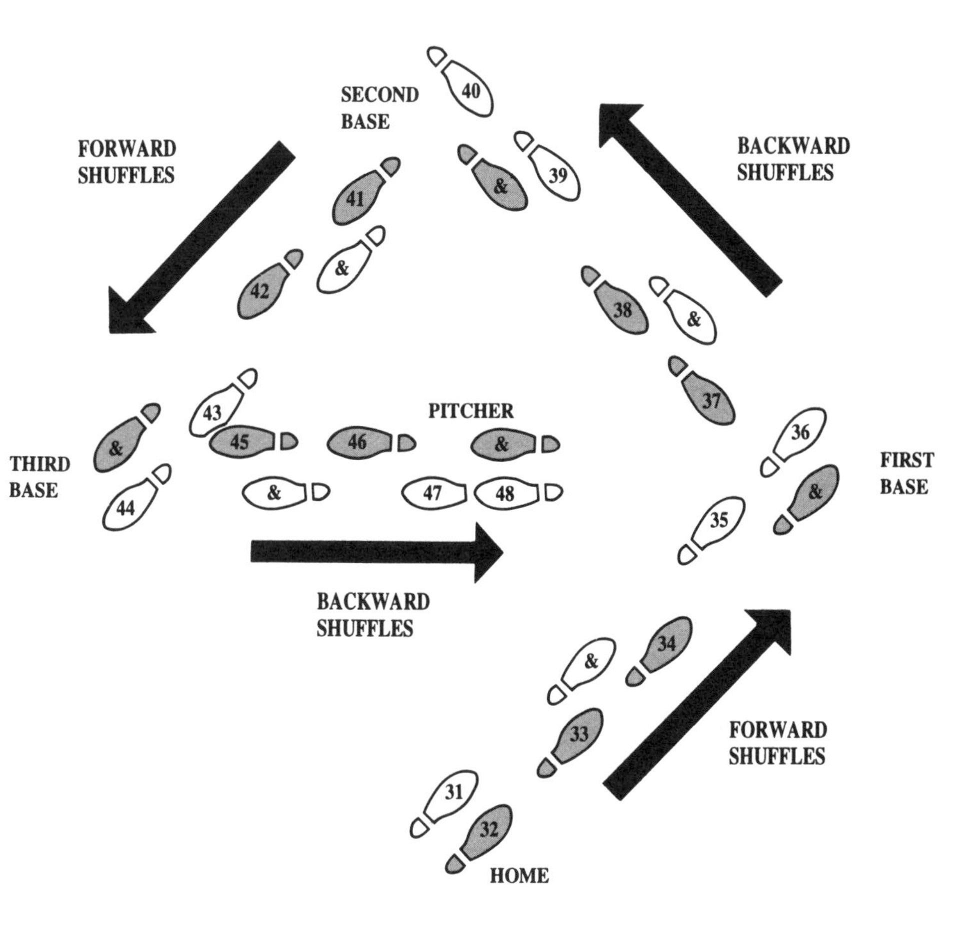

SHUFFLE PATTERN FOR REGGAE COWBOY II

Shuffle forward from "home plate" to "first base"

33-34 Right shuffle diagonally forward with 1/8 turn right
- 33 Step **right** foot diagonally forward and pivot 1/8 turn right
- & Step **left** foot next to **right** foot
- 34 Step **right** foot forward

35-36 Left shuffle forward with 1/4 turn right
- 35 Step **left** foot forward
- & Step **right** foot next to **left** foot
- 36 Step **left** foot forward and pivot 1/4 turn right

Shuffle backward to "second base"

37-38 Right shuffle back
- 37 Step **right** foot back
- & Step **left** foot next to **right** foot
- 38 Step **right** foot back

39-40 Left shuffle back with 1/4 turn right
- 39 Step **left** foot back
- & Step **right** foot next to **left** foot
- 40 Step **left** foot back and pivot 1/4 turn right

Shuffle forward to "third base"

41-42 Right shuffle forward
- 41 Step **right** foot forward
- & Step **left** foot next to **right** foot
- 42 Step **right** foot forward

43-44 Left shuffle forward with 1/8 turn right
- 43 Step **left** foot forward
- & Step **right** foot next to **left** foot
- 44 Step **left** foot forward and pivot 1/8 turn right

Shuffle backward to "pitcher's mound"

45-46 Right shuffle back
- 45 Step **right** foot back
- & Step **left** foot next to **right** foot
- 46 Step **right** foot back

47-48 Left shuffle back
- 47 Step **left** foot back
- & Step **right** foot next to **left** foot
- 48 Step **left** foot back

Repeat Pattern

Variation

Some dancers replace one or more of the step-slide-step-slide patterns (beats 17-32) with "three-step turns with touches". For example, replacing the step-slide-step-slide patterns on beats 25-32 would look like:

25-28 Three-step turn to right with left touch
- 25 Step **right** foot to right side and pivot $\frac{1}{2}$ turn right
- 26 Step **left** foot to left side and pivot $\frac{1}{2}$ turn right
- 27 Step **right** foot to right side
- 28 Touch **left** foot next to **right** foot

29-32 Three-step turn to left with right touch
- 29 Step **left** foot to left side and pivot $\frac{1}{2}$ turn left
- 30 Step **right** foot to right side and pivot $\frac{1}{2}$ turn left
- 31 Step **left** foot to left side
- 32 Touch **right** foot next to **left** foot

Rhythm Line:

```
secs      .....1.....2.....3.....4.....5.....6.....7.....8.....9....10
120 bpm     1 & 2  3 & 4  1 & 2  3 & 4  1  2  3  4  1  2  3  4  1  2  3  4
foot        R . .  L . .  R . .  L . .  R  L  R  L  L  R  L  R  R  L  R  L
other         cc     cc     cc     cc
            (claps)

secs      ....11....12....13....14....15....16....17....18....19....20
120 bpm     1  2  3  4  1  2  3  4  1  2  3  4  1 &2  3 &4  1 &2  3 &4
foot        L  R  L  R  R  L  R  L  L  R  L  R  R LR  L RL  R LR  L RL

secs      ....21....22....23....24....25....26....27....28....29....30
120 bpm     1 & 2  3 & 4  1 & 2  3 & 4  1 & 2  3 & 4  1 & 2  3 & 4  1  2  3  4
foot        R L R  L R L  R L R  L R L  Repeat Pattern
```

Cues:

right / clap-clap / left / clap-clap
right / clap-clap / left / clap-clap
back / back / back / hitch
back / back / back / hitch
right / slide / right / touch
left / slide / left / touch
right / slide / right / touch
left / slide / left / touch
turn-together-right / left-together-turn
back-together-back / back-together-turn
right-together-right / left-together-turn
back-together-back / back-together-back

Cajun Slap

About this dance: "Cajun" is a label applied to southern Louisianans of Acadian French descent. Cajuns have produced a distinctive culture in which their English dialect, style of cooking and, of course, form of music all play a part. Marked by its high energy and clear fiddle presence, Cajun music makes many want to dance. Cajun Slap is most fun when danced to music of this type (for example, "Down At The Twist And Shout").

I DON'T MIND PLAYIN' "CAJUN SLAP" FOR THEM, BUT I SURE WISH THEY'D SLAP ON THE BEAT!

The Dance

Difficulty Level: III **Choreographer:** Unknown

Dance Faces: two directions **Pattern Length**: 40 Beats

Suggested Music:

For practicing – "Walkin' Away A Winner" by Kathy Mattea (Track 1 on your ***Free CD***).

For dancing – "The South's Gonna Do It" – originally recorded by Charlie Daniels Band (Track 6 on your ***Free CD***). "Down At The Twist And Shout" by Mary Chapin Carpenter.

Beats	Description
	Vines and Touches
1-4	Right vine with left touch
	1 Step **right** foot to right side
	2 Step **left** foot behind **right** foot
	3 Step **right** foot to right side
	4 Touch **left** foot next to **right** foot
5	Touch **left** foot to left side
6	Touch **left** foot next to **right** foot
7	Touch **left** foot to left side
8	Touch **left** foot next to **right** foot
9-12	Left vine with right touch
	9 Step **left** foot to left side
	10 Step **right** foot behind **left** foot
	11 Step **left** foot to left side
	12 Touch **right** foot next to **left** foot
13	Touch **right** foot to right side
14	Touch **right** foot next to **left** foot
15	Touch **right** foot to right side
16	Step **right** foot next to **left** foot
	Toe Struts
17-18	Left toe strut forward
	17 Touch **left** toe forward
	18 Lower **left** heel (step **left** foot down)
19-20	Right toe strut forward
	19 Touch **right** toe forward
	20 Lower **right** heel (step **right** foot down)
21-22	Left toe strut forward
	21 Touch **left** toe forward
	22 Lower **left** heel (step **left** foot down)

23-24 Right toe strut forward
  23 Touch **right** toe forward
  24 Lower **right** heel (step **right** foot down)

Touches and Slaps

25 Touch **left** heel forward
26 Touch **left** heel forward
27 Touch **left** toe back
28 Touch **left** toe back

29 Touch **left** heel forward
30 Hitch **left** leg and slap **left** knee with right hand
31 Touch **left** heel forward
32 Hitch **left** leg and slap **left** heel with right hand

Step-Slide, Turn and Slap

33 Step **left** foot forward
34 Slide **right** foot next to **left** foot
35 Step **left** foot forward
36 Scuff **right** foot

37-38 Military turn to the left
  37 Step **right** foot forward
  38 Pivot on **both** feet ½ turn left

39 Touch **right** toe to right side
40 Hook **right** leg behind **left** leg and slap **right** heel with left hand

Repeat Pattern

Rhythm Line:

```
secs      .....1.....2.....3.....4.....5.....6.....7.....8.....9....10
180 bpm    1 2 3 4 1 2 3 4 1 2 3 4 1 2 3 4 1 2 3 4 1 2 3 4 1 2 3 4 1 2
foot       R L R L L L L L L R L R R R R R L L R R L L R R L L L L L L
other                                                                s
                                                                (slap)

secs     ....11....12....13....14....15....16....17....18....19....20
180 bpm   3 4 1 2 3 4 1 2 3 4 1 2 3 4 1 2 3 4 1 2 3 4 1 2 3 4 1 2 3 4
foot      L L L R L R R B R R
other       s               s
```

Cues:

right / behind / right / touch
side / together / side / together
left / behind / left / touch
side / together / side / together
toe / heel / toe / heel
toe / heel / toe / heel
heel / heel / toe / toe
heel / slap / heel / slap
step / slide / step / scuff
step / turn / side / slap

Cowboy Charleston

About this dance: This dance is also known as Charleston Tap and the Charleston Cha Cha. It is a Country and Western version of the roaring twenties flapper favorite. Isn't that the cat's pajamas!

New Concepts, Steps and Combinations

New Combinations

Charleston Step

Instructs you to make eight movements in four beats of music, beginning on a ½ beat. The pattern involves each foot swinging forward and back. The foot which leads (begins) the pattern will be specified. On the ½ beat before beat one, the lead foot is lifted slightly off the floor and is swung out to the side and forward. On "1", the lead foot touches forward. On "&", the lead foot is swung out to the side and back. On "2", the lead foot steps back. On "&", the following foot is swung out to the side and back. On "3", the following foot touches back. On "&", the following foot is swung out to the side and forward. On "4", the following foot steps forward. When done to music, these eight movements have the appearance of legs swinging smoothly from one position to the next.

For example, "right Charleston step" instructs you to swing your right foot out to the right side and forward, touch your right foot forward, swing your right foot out to the side and back, step your right foot back, swing your left foot out to the left side and back, touch your left foot back, swing your left foot out to the left side and forward, and step forward on your left foot. These movements are done to a count of "and one and two and three and four."

In addition to foot movements, the charleston step has arm movements that accompany it. Throughout the eight movements, the arms are essentially opposite one another (for example, if the right arm is forward, the left arm is back). On the ½ beats the arms are out to the sides. On the full beats, the arm opposite the lead foot is forward when the lead foot is forward and is back when the lead foot is back. As with the feet, when done to music, these eight movements have the appearance of arms swinging smoothly from one position to the next.

For example, "right Charleston step" instructs you to swing your arms out to the sides, left arm forward, to the sides, left arm back, to the sides, left arm forward, to the sides, left arm back.
For a very advanced Charleston look, swivel your heels alternately out and in to a syncopated rhythm. (We have never seen this done on a Country and Western dance floor.)

Sailor step Instructs you to make three foot movements in two beats of music. The foot to lead (begin) the pattern, and whether it steps across or behind, will be specified. On beat one, the lead foot steps across or behind the following foot. On the ½ beat, the following foot steps to the side. On beat two, the lead foot steps to the side. When a sailor step is completed, the feet are about shoulder width apart. In a sailor step, the body leans slightly in the direction of the foot to move first.

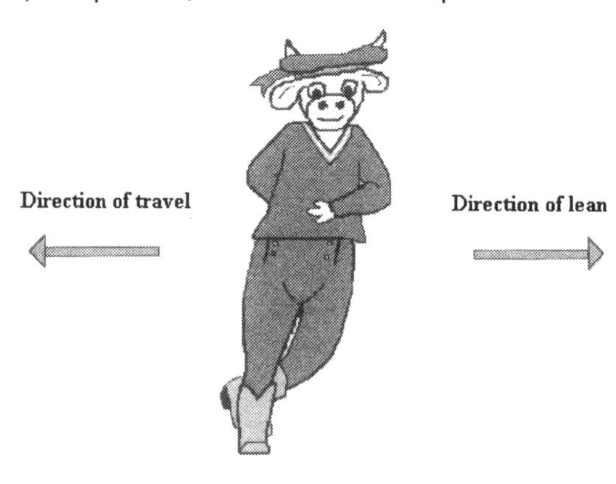

For example, "right sailor step (begin behind)" instructs you to step your right foot behind your left, step your left foot to the left side and step your right foot to the right side. These movements are done to a count of "one and two". Throughout a right sailor step, you would lean slightly to the right.

The Dance

Difficulty Level: III

Choreographer: Unknown

Dance Faces: four directions

Pattern Length: 20 Steps

Suggested Music:

For practicing – "Walkin' Away A Winner" by Kathy Mattea (Track 1 on your ***Free CD***).

For dancing – "Redneck Girl" – originally recorded by Bellamy Brothers (Track 11 on your ***Free CD***). "Sold" by John Michael Montgomery.

Beats	Description	
	Charleston Steps	
1-4	Right Charleston step	
	&	Swing **right** leg to right side and forward
	1	Touch **right** foot forward
	&	Swing **right** leg to right side and back
	2	Step **right** foot back
	&	Swing **left** leg to left side and back
	3	Touch **left** foot back
	&	Swing **left** leg to left side and forward
	4	Step **left** foot forward

5- 8 Right Charleston step
- & Swing **right** leg to right side and forward
- 5 Touch **right** foot forward
- & Swing **right** leg to right side and back
- 6 Step **right** foot back
- & Swing **left** leg to left side and back
- 7 Touch **left** foot back
- & Swing **left** leg to left side and forward
- 8 Step **left** foot forward

Sailor Steps and Turn

9 Touch **right** toe to right side
10 Touch **right** toe to right side

11-12 Right sailor step (begin behind)
- 11 Step **right** foot behind **left** foot
- & Step **left** foot to left side
- 12 Step **right** foot to right side

13 Touch **left** toe to left side
14 Touch **left** toe to left side

15-16 Right sailor step (begin behind) with 1/4 turn right
- 15 Step **left** foot behind **right** foot
- & Step **right** foot to right side and pivot 1/4 turn right
- 16 Step **left** foot to left side

Repeat Pattern

Rhythm Line:

```
secs      .....1.....2.....3.....4.....5.....6.....7.....8.....9....10
120 bpm   &1 &2 &3 &4 &1 &2 &3 &4  1  2  3 &4  1  2  3 &4 &1 &2 &3 &4
foot      RR RR LL LL RR RR LL LL  R  R  R LR  L  L  L RL  Repeat Pattern
```

Cues:

and-forward-and-back-and-back-and-forward
and-forward-and-back-and-back-and-forward
toe / toe / behind-side-side
toe / toe / behind-turn-side

Sunflower

About this dance: Looking at the steps, this is an easy dance with a simple pattern: stomp once, twice, thrice and then kick once, twice, thrice. But, looking and doing are two different things. Except for the steps back, your weight is on your left leg all the time. We particularly like "Bubba Shot the Juke Box" for this dance. It moves!

New Concepts, Steps and Combinations

New Steps

Flick Instructs you to kick the identified foot backward. In a flick, the toe points down.

The Dance

Difficulty Level: III

Choreographer: Unknown

Dance Faces: four directions

Pattern Length: 30 beats

Suggested Music:

For practicing – "Talk Some" – originally recorded by Billy Ray Cyrus (Track 3 on your ***Free CD***).

For dancing – "The South's Gonna Do It" – originally recorded by Charlie Daniels Band (Track 6 on your ***Free CD***). "Bubba Shot the JukeBox" by Mark Chestnut; "Boom! It Was Over" by Robert Ellis Orrall.

Beats	Description
	Forward and Back with One, Two, and Three Stomps
1	Step **left** foot forward
2	Stomp-up **right** foot forward
3	Step **right** foot back
4	Touch **left** foot next to **right** foot
5	Step **left** foot forward
6	Stomp-up **right** foot forward
7	Stomp-up **right** foot diagonally forward

8	Step **right** foot back
9	Touch **left** foot next to **right** foot
10	Step **left** foot forward
11	Stomp-up **right** foot forward
12	Stomp-up **right** foot diagonally forward
13	Stomp-up **right** foot forward
14	Step **right** foot back
15	Touch **left** foot next to **right** foot

Forward and Back with One, Two, and Three Kicks

16	Step **left** foot forward
17	Kick **right** foot forward and clap
18	Step **right** foot back
19	Touch **left** foot next to **right** foot
20	Step **left** foot forward
21	Kick **right** foot forward and clap
22	Kick **right** foot forward and clap
23	Step **right** foot back
24	Touch **left** foot next to **right** foot
25	Step **left** foot forward
26	Kick **right** foot forward and clap
27	Flick **right** foot back and pivot on **left** foot ¼ turn left
28	Kick **right** foot forward and clap
29	Step **right** foot back
30	Touch **left** foot next to **right** foot

Repeat Pattern

Rhythm Line:

```
secs     .....1.....2.....3.....4.....5.....6.....7.....8.....9....10
180 bpm   1 2 3 4 1 2 3 4 1 2 3 4 1 2 3 4 1 2 3 4 1 2 3 4 1 2 3 4 1 2
foot      L R R L L R R R L L R R R R L L R R L L R R R L L R R R R L Repeat
other                                     c       c c       c   c
                                        (clap)
```

Cues:

forward / stomp / back / touch
forward / stomp / stomp / back / touch
forward / stomp / stomp / stomp / back / touch
forward / kick / back / touch
forward / kick / kick / back / touch
forward / kick / turn / kick / back / touch

Lobo

About this dance: Lobo is most often done to fast music. Our favorite music for this dance is "The South's Gonna Do It" – originally recorded by Charlie Daniels Band. If you begin dancing after the eighth measure of music (i.e. on beat 33), your last stomp in the pattern occurs just as the song ends. Very impressive! For styling, we have suggested a sequence of hand positions for the hand claps. If you prefer, you may do all of the hand claps at the same height.

The Dance

Difficulty Level: III

Choreographer: Unknown

Dance Faces: four directions

Pattern Length: 28 Beats

Suggested Music:

For practicing – "Walkin' Away a Winner" by Kathy Mattea (Track 1 on your ***Free CD***).

For dancing – "The South's Gonna Do It" – originally recorded by Charlie Daniels Band (Track 6 on your ***Free CD***). "Ain't Goin' Down 'Til The Sun Comes Up" by Garth Brooks.

Beats	Description
	Touches and Scuffs
1	Touch **left** heel forward
2	Touch **left** toe back
3	Scuff **left** foot
4	Step **left** foot next to **right** foot
5	Touch **right** heel forward
6	Touch **right** toe back
7	Scuff **right** foot
8	Step **right** foot next to **left** foot
	Military Turns
9-10	Military turn to the right
	9 Step **left** foot forward
	10 Pivot on **both** feet ½ turn right
11-12	Military turn to the right
	11 Step **left** foot forward
	12 Pivot on **both** feet ½ turn right

Vine and Turn

13-16 Left vine with right hitch and ¼ turn right
- 13 Step **left** foot to left side
- 14 Step **right** foot behind **left** foot
- 15 Step **left** foot to left side
- 16 Hitch **right** leg and pivot on **left** foot ¼ turn right

Walk Back and Forward with Claps

17 Step **right** foot back
18 Step **left** foot back
19 Step **right** foot back
20 Touch **left** toe next to **right** foot and clap
(Clap hands to left side at waist height)

21 Step **left** foot forward
22 Touch **right** toe next to **left** foot and clap
(Clap hands to right side at shoulder height)
23 Step **right** foot forward
24 Touch **left** toe next to **right** foot and clap
(Clap hands to left side above your head)

Kicks and Stomps

25 Kick **left** foot forward
26 Kick **left** foot forward
27 Stomp **left** foot next to **right** foot
28 Stomp **right** foot next to **left** foot

Repeat Pattern

Rhythm Line:

```
secs     .....1.....2.....3.....4.....5.....6.....7.....8.....9....10
180 bpm  1 2 3 4 1 2 3 4 1 2 3 4 1 2 3 4 1 2 3 4 1 2 3 4 1 2 3 4 1 2
foot     L L L L R R R R L B L B L R L R R L R L L R R L L L L R Repeat
other                                          c   c   c
                                            (clap)
```

Cues:

heel / toe / scuff / together
heel / toe / scuff / together
step / turn / step / turn
left / behind / left / turn
back / back / back / touch
left / touch / right / touch
kick / kick / stomp / stomp

Alley Cat

About this dance: Several dances share the name of Alley Cat. This is the version done in our region.

New Concepts, Steps and Combinations

New Concept

Shimmy Describes an upper body movement in which the shoulders alternately are moved forward and backward in syncopated rhythm (i.e. on beats and half-beats).

For example, "beats 1-4 Shimmy shoulders" tells you to: on beat one, move your right shoulder forward (left goes back), on "and" move your left shoulder forward, on beat two, move your right shoulder forward, on "and" move left shoulder forward, and so on.

Dance descriptions may call for shimmies with or without foot movements. Some individuals, particularly men, inadvertently do hip wiggles instead of shimmies and these hip movements may interfere with foot movements. Thus, alternatives to shimmies, which do not interfere with foot movements, may be offered as "variations".

New Step

Draw-up Instructs you to slide the identified foot for a designated number of beats. The action is continuous, but slow. This move produces a look of the foot being pulled from one position to the next. When a draw-up is completed, the drawn foot is touching the floor but bears no weight. A draw-up is similar in movement to a slide-up: they differ only in that a slide-up is completed in one beat of music. Note that a draw is different from a draw-up. In a draw, the sliding foot bears weight; in a draw-up, it does not.

For example, "beats 1-3 Draw-up **left** foot next to **right** foot" specifies a three beat draw-up of the left foot. On beat one, you would begin to slide your left foot toward your right, and you would continue this motion through beat two. On beat three, the draw is completed with the left foot touching the floor next to the right foot.

The Dance

Difficulty Level: III

Choreographer: Donna Aiken

Dance Faces: four directions

Pattern Length: 64 Beats

Suggested Music:

For practicing – "I Wanna Go Too Far" – originally recorded by Trisha Yearwood (Track 4 on your ***Free CD***).

For dancing – "Shut Up And Kiss Me" – originally recorded by Mary Chapin Carpenter (Track 8 on your ***Free CD***). "Trashy Women" by Confederate Railroad.

Beats	Description
	Heel Splits and Touches
1- 2	Heel Split 1 Move heels apart 2 Return heels to center
3- 4	Heel Split 3 Move heels apart 4 Return heels to center
5	Touch **right** heel forward
6	Touch **right** foot next to **left** foot
7	Touch **right** heel forward
8	Step **right** foot next to **left** foot
9-10	Heel Split 9 Move heels apart 10 Return heels to center
11-12	Heel Split 11 Move heels apart 12 Return heels to center
13	Touch **left** heel forward
14	Touch **left** foot next to **right** foot
15	Touch **left** heel forward
16	Touch **left** foot next to **right** foot
	Diagonal Step-Slides and Claps
17	Step **left** foot diagonally forward
18	Slide **right** foot next to **left** foot and clap
19	Step **left** foot diagonally forward
20	Slide **right** foot next to **left** foot and clap

21	Step **left** foot diagonally forward
22	Slide **right** foot next to **left** foot and clap
23	Step **left** foot diagonally forward
24	Slide-up **right** foot next to **left** foot and clap

Diagonally Back and Clap

25	Step **right** foot diagonally back
26	Touch **left** foot next to **right** foot and clap
27	Step **left** foot diagonally back
28	Touch **right** foot next to **left** foot and clap
29	Step **right** foot diagonally back
30	Touch **left** foot next to **right** foot and clap
31	Step **left** foot diagonally back
32	Touch **right** foot next to **left** foot and clap

Shimmies to the Right

33	Step **right** foot to right while shimmying
34-36	Draw **left** foot next to **right** foot while shimmying
37	Step **right** foot to right while shimmying
38-40	Draw-up **left** foot next to **right** foot while shimmying

Shimmies to the Left

41	Step **left** foot to right while shimmying
42-44	Draw **right** foot next to **left** foot while shimmying
45	Step **left** foot to right while shimmying
46-48	Draw-up **right** foot next to **left** foot while shimmying

Kick-Ball-Changes and Touches

49-50 Right kick-ball-change
- 49 Kick **right** foot forward
- & Step ball of **right** foot next to **left** foot
- 50 Step **left** foot in place

51-52 Right kick-ball-change
- 51 Kick **right** foot forward
- & Step ball of **right** foot next to **left** foot
- 52 Step **left** foot in place

53	Step **right** foot forward
54	Touch **left** toe next to **right** foot
55	Touch **left** toe to left side
56	Touch **left** toe next to **right** foot

Vine and Back

57-60 Left vine with 1/4 turn left and right stomp
- 57 Step **left** foot to left side
- 58 Step **right** foot behind **left** foot
- 59 Step **left** foot to left side and pivot 1/4 turn left
- 60 Stomp-up **right** foot next to **left** foot

61	Step **right** foot back
62	Step **left** foot back
63	Step **right** foot back
64	Stomp **left** foot next to **right** foot

Repeat Pattern

Variation

Some dancers prefer to do left heel swivels instead of the heel splits (Beats 1-4 and 9-12).

Rhythm Line:

```
secs        .....1.....2.....3.....4.....5.....6.....7.....8.....9....10
120 bpm       1  2  3  4  1  2  3  4  1  2  3  4  1  2  3  4  1  2  3  4
foot          B  B  B  B  R  R  R  R  B  B  B  B  L  L  L  L  L  R  L  R
other                                                            c     c
                                                              (clap)

secs        ....11....12....13....14....15....16....17....18....19....20
120 bpm       1  2  3  4  1  2  3  4  1  2  3  4  1  2  3  4  1  2  3  4
foot          L  R  L  R  R  L  L  R  R  L  L  R  R  -  L  -  R  -  L  -
other            c     c     c     c     c     c   shimmies    shimmies


secs        ....21....22....23....24....25....26....27....28....29....30
120 bpm       1  2  3  4  1  2  3  4  1 & 2  3 & 4  1  2  3  4  1  2  3  4
foot          L  -  R  -  L  -  R  -  R R L  R R L  R  L  L  L  L  R  L  R
other           shimmies    shimmies

secs        ....31....32....33....34....35....36....37....38....39....40
120 bpm       1  2  3  4  1  2  3  4  1  2  3  4  1  2  3  4  1  2  3  4
foot          R  L  R  L  Repeat Pattern
other

NOTE:  - L - denotes a 3 count draw of the left foot
```

Cues:

apart / together / apart / together
heel / touch / heel / together
apart / together / apart / together
heel / touch / heel / touch
step / slide / step / slide
step / slide / step / touch
back / touch / back / touch
back / touch / back / touch
right / shimmy / shimmy / together
right / shimmy / shimmy / touch
left / shimmy / shimmy / together
left / shimmy / shimmy / touch
kick-ball-change / kick-ball-change
forward / touch / touch / touch
left / behind / turn / stomp
back / back / back / stomp

Watermelon Crawl

About this dance: This dance was choreographed to accompany the song "Watermelon Crawl" by Tracy Byrd.

New Concepts, Steps and Combinations

New Combinations

Alternating Knee Pops Instructs you to sequentially flex and straighten the knees, alternating left and right, for the designated number of beats. The knee that flexes first (lead knee) will be specified in the instruction. On beat one, bend the lead knee by lifting the heel of that foot off the floor. On beat two, bend the following knee (by lifting its heel off the floor) and straighten the lead knee (by lowering its heel). On beat three, bend the lead knee and straighten the following knee. Continue this sequence of movements for the designated number of beats. Note that at the end of this sequence, one of the heels will remain lifted off the floor.

For example, "beats 1-4 Alternating knee pops (begin left)" instructs you to: on "1", bend left knee (raise left heel); on "2", bend right knee (raise right heel) and straighten left knee (lower left heel); on "3", bend left knee (raise left heel) and straighten right knee (lower right heel); on "4", bend right knee (raise right heel) and straighten left knee (lower left heel).

Cha Cha Instructs you to take three small steps to two beats of music. The foot which leads the combination, as well as the direction (right, left, forward, back, in place, etc.), will be specified in the dance description.

For example, "right Cha Cha forward" instructs you to: on "1", step forward on your right foot; on "&", step forward on your left foot; on "2", step forward on your right foot.

A Cha Cha is much like a shuffle: both have three steps to a two beat, syncopated rhythm. However, in a Cha Cha the three steps are all the same size, whereas, in a shuffle, the second step is shorter than the first and third. Because there is no travelling in a "shuffle in place" or "Cha Cha in place", the "in place" versions of these combinations look identical.

Charleston Kick Instructs you to make four movements to four beats of music. The foot that begins (leads) the combination is specified. On beat one, the lead foot steps forward. On beat two, the following foot kicks forward. On beat three, the following foot steps back, and, on beat four, the lead foot touches back.

For example, "Right Charleston kick" instructs you: on "1", step your right foot forward; on "2", kick your left foot forward; on "3", step back on your left foot; on "4", touch your right toe back.
For a very advanced Charleston look, swivel your heels alternately out and in to a syncopated rhythm. (We have never seen this done on a Country and Western dance floor.)

Sugar Foot Instructs you to make a heel and toe touch of a designated foot to two beats of music. In the sugar foot, sometimes the heel touches first and sometimes the toe touches first: the order will be specified in the dance description. The heel and toe touches are both done next to the weighted foot. On the heel touches, the sugar foot is turned out. On the toe touches, the sugar foot is turned in.

For example, "Right toe-heel sugar foot" instructs you to, on "1", touch your right toe next to your left foot (right foot turned in), and on "2", touch your right heel next to your left foot (right foot turned out).

The Dance

Difficulty Level: III

Choreographer: Sue Lipscomb

Dance Faces: four directions

Pattern Length: 40 Beats

Suggested Music:

For practicing – "I Wanna Go Too Far" – originally recorded by Trisha Yearwood (Track 4 on your ***Free CD***).

For dancing – "Redneck Girl" – originally recorded by Bellamy Brothers (Track 11 on your ***Free CD***). "Watermelon Crawl" by Tracy Byrd.

Beats	Description
	Touches and Cha Chas
1- 2	Right toe-heel sugar foot
	1 Touch **right** toe *(foot turned in)* next to **left** foot
	2 Touch **right** heel *(foot turned in)* next to **left** foot
3- 4	Right Cha Cha in place
	3 Step **right** foot home
	& Step **left** foot in place
	4 Step **right** foot in place
5-6	Left toe-heel sugar foot
	5 Touch **left** toe *(foot turned in)* next to **right** foot
	6 Touch **left** heel *(foot turned in)* next to **right** foot

7-8 Left Cha Cha in place
- 7 Step **left** foot home
- & Step **right** foot in place
- 8 Step **left** foot in place

Charleston Kicks

9-12 Right Charleston kick
- 9 Step **right** foot forward
- 10 Kick **left** foot forward
- 11 Step **left** foot back
- 12 Touch **right** toe back

13-16 Right Charleston kick
- 13 Step **right** foot forward
- 14 Kick **left** foot forward
- 15 Step **left** foot back
- 16 Touch **right** toe back

Vines

17-20 Right vine with left touch
- 17 Step **right** foot to right side
- 18 Step **left** foot behind **right** foot
- 19 Step **right** foot to right side
- 20 Touch **left** foot next to **right** foot

21-24 Left vine with ¼ turn left and right touch
- 21 Step **left** foot to left side
- 22 Step **right** foot behind **left** foot
- 23 Step **left** foot to left side and pivot ¼ turn left
- 24 Touch **right** foot next to **left** foot

Steps and Draws

25 Step **right** foot diagonally forward (Step as far diagonally forward as you can.)

26-28 Draw-up **left** foot next to **right** foot (and clap on beat 28)

29 Step **left** foot diagonally back (Step as far diagonally back as you can.)

30-32 Draw-up **right** foot next to **left** foot (and clap on beat 32)

Knee Pops

33-36 Alternating knee pops (begin left)
- 33 Bend **left** knee
- 34 Bend **right** knee and straighten **left** knee
- 35 Bend **left** knee and straighten **right** knee
- 36 Bend **right** knee and straighten **left** knee

Military Turns

37-38 Military turn to the left
- 37 Step **right** foot forward
- 38 Pivot on **both** feet ½ turn left

39-40 Military turn to the left
- 39 Step **right** foot forward
- 40 Pivot on **both** feet ½ turn left

Repeat Pattern

Variation

Some dancers, particularly women, add shoulder shimmies to the steps and draws on beats 25-32.

Rhythm Line:

```
secs      .....1.....2.....3.....4.....5.....6.....7.....8.....9....10
120 bpm    1   2   3 &4   1   2   3 &4   1   2   3   4   1   2   3   4   1   2   3   4
foot       R   R   R LR   L   L   L RL   R   L   L   R   R   L   L   R   R   L   R   L
other

secs      ....11....12....13....14....15....16....17....18....19....20
120 bpm    1   2   3   4   1   2   3   4   1   2   3   4   1   2   3   4   1   2   3   4
foot       L   R   L   R   R   L   -   -   L   R   -   -   .   .   .   .   R   B   R   B
other                          draw    c       draw    c   p   p   p   p
                                    (clap)              (knee pops)
```

Cues:

toe / heel / Cha-Cha-Cha
toe / heel / Cha-Cha-Cha
right / kick / back / touch
right / kick / back / touch
right / behind / right / touch
left / behind / turn / touch
right / draw / draw / clap
left / draw / draw / clap
pop / pop / pop / pop
step / turn / step / turn

Berlin Boogie

About this dance: This is an older dance that is fun to do, particularly to fast music. We have heard of "unofficial contests" to determine who can do this dance the fastest.

New Concepts, Steps and Combinations

New Combination

Travelling Sugar Foot Specifies either a right or left sideways movement in two beats of music. In a travelling sugar foot, the leg opposite the direction to be travelled supports the weight alternately on heel and toe, while the other leg does a heel-toe sugar foot. On beat one, the weighted foot swivels its toe in the direction of travel. At the same time, the other heel touches, also with toe pointed in the direction of travel, next to the weighted foot. On beat two, the weighted foot swivels its heel in the direction of travel. At the same time, the other toe is touched, also with heel pointed in the direction of travel, next to the weighted foot. Note, on each beat, both feet will be pointed in the same direction. This combination produces a look of gliding across the floor. Most dancers find this move to be very awkward at first. It gets much easier with practice.

For example, "travelling sugar foot to the right" instructs you, on beat one, to swivel your left toe to the right and touch your right heel next to your left foot, so that both toes will be pointed diagonally right; on beat two, swivel your left heel to the right and touch your right toe next to your left foot so that both toes point diagonally left.

The Dance

Difficulty Level: III
Choreographer: Unknown
Dance Faces: four directions
Pattern Length: 32 Beats
Suggested Music:

For practicing – "The City Put The Country Back In Me" – originally recorded by Neal McCoy (Track 2 on your ***Free CD***).

For dancing – "The South's Gonna Do It" – originally recorded by Charlie Daniels Band (Track 6 on your ***Free CD***). "I Got it Bad" by Colin Ray. "Gonna Get A Life" by Mark Chestnut.

Beats	Description
	Heel Touches
1	Touch **left** heel forward
2	Step **left** foot next to **right** foot
3	Touch **right** heel forward
4	Step **right** foot next to **left** foot
5	Touch **left** heel forward
6	Step **left** foot next to **right** foot
	Travelling Sugar Feet
7- 8	Travelling sugar foot to the right
	7 Swivel **left** toe to right and touch **right** heel *(foot turned in)* next to **left** foot
	8 Swivel **left** heel to right and touch **right** toe *(foot turned in)* next to **left** foot
9-10	Travelling sugar foot to the right
	9 Swivel **left** toe to right and touch **right** heel *(foot turned in)* next to **left** foot
	10 Swivel **left** heel to right and touch **right** toe *(foot turned in)* next to **left** foot
11-12	Travelling sugar foot to the right
	11 Swivel **left** toe to right and touch **right** heel next to **left** foot
	12 Swivel **left** heel to right and touch **right** toe next to **left** foot
	Touches
13	Touch **right** heel forward
14	Touch **right** heel forward
15	Touch **right** toe back
16	Touch **right** toe back
	Shuffles
17-18	Right shuffle forward
	17 Step **right** foot forward
	& Step **left** foot next to **right** foot
	18 Step **right** foot forward
19-20	Left shuffle forward
	19 Step **left** foot forward
	& Step **right** foot next to **left** foot
	20 Step **left** foot forward

21-22 Right shuffle forward
- 21 Step **right** foot forward
- & Step **left** foot next to **right** foot
- 22 Step **right** foot forward

23-24 Left shuffle forward
- 23 Step **left** foot forward
- & Step **right** foot next to **left** foot
- 24 Step **left** foot forward

Jazz Boxes

25-28 Right jazz box with ¼ turn right and left step
- 25 Step **right** foot across **left** foot
- 26 Step **left** foot back
- 27 Step **right** foot to right side and pivot ¼ turn right
- 28 Step **left** foot next to **right** foot

29-32 Right jazz box with left stomp-up
- 29 Step **right** foot across **left** foot
- 30 Step **left** foot back
- 31 Step **right** foot to right side
- 32 Stomp-up **left** foot next to **right** foot

Repeat Pattern

Variation

Some dancers prefer toe struts to shuffles on beats 17-24. We think that the struts are a better match to the style of the travelling sugar foot.

17-18 Right toe strut forward
- 17 Touch **right** toe forward
- 18 Lower **right** heel (step **right** foot down)

19-20 Left toe strut forward
- 19 Touch **left** toe forward
- 20 Lower **left** heel (step **left** foot down)

For beats 21-24, do another right and left toe strut.

Rhythm Line:

```
secs      .....1.....2.....3.....4.....5.....6.....7.....8.....9....10
180 bpm    1 2 3 4 1 2 3 4 1 2 3 4 1 2 3 4 1&2 3&4 1&2 3&4 1 2 3 4 1 2
foot       L L R R L L B B B B B B R R R R RLR LRL RLR LRL R L R L R L

secs      ....11....12....13....14....15....16....17....18....19....20
180 bpm    3 4 1 2 3 4 1 2 3 4 1 2 3 4 1 2 3 4 1&2 3&4 1&2 3&4 1 2 3 4
foot       R L  Repeat Pattern
```

Cues:

heel / together / heel / together / heel / together
heels / toes / heels / toes / heels / toes
heel / heel / toe / toe
right-together-right/left-together-left
right-together-right/left-together-left
cross / back / turn / together
cross / back / side / stomp

Level IV

Applejack

About this dance: Applejack is also called Crazy Feet, presumably because of the foot movements. The dance involves pivoting on the ball of one foot and the heel of the other. Learning this dance is like trying to pat your head and rub your tummy at the same time. The dance can be done to fast music, but moderate music makes it easier.

New Concepts, Steps and Combinations

New Step

Jump Instructs you to jump in the specified direction, lifting off of and landing on both feet. Jumps are done to one beat of music.

New Combination

Swivet Instructs you to swivel both feet, on the heel of one and ball of the other. Both feet turn approximately 45 degrees in the direction specified and then back to center in two beats of music. The direction of the swivet identifies the direction your toes will point on the first movement. The foot named in the direction of the swivet swivels its toe and the other foot swivels its heel. While swiveling, your weight will be on the heel of one foot and the ball of the other. At the completion of a swivet, both feet will be centered under your body and flat on the floor.

For example, "swivet to right" instructs you to: on "1", swivel your right toe to the right and your left heel to the left; on "2", swivel your right toe to center and your left heel to center.

The Dance

Difficulty Level: IV

Choreographer: Unknown

Dance Faces: four directions

Pattern Length: 26 Beats

Suggested Music:

For practicing – "The City Put The Country Back In Me" – originally recorded by Neal McCoy (Track 2 on your ***Free CD***).

For dancing – "The South's Gonna Do It" – originally recorded by Charlie Daniels Band (Track 6 on your ***Free CD***). "I Don't Need Your Rockin' Chair" by George Jones. "I Fell In The Water That You Walked On" by John Anderson.

Beats	Description
	Swivets
1- 2	Swivet to left
	1 Swivel **left** toe to left and swivel **right** heel to right
	2 Swivel **left** toe to center and swivel **right** heel to center
3- 4	Swivet to right
	3 Swivel **right** toe to right and swivel **left** heel to left
	4 Swivel **right** toe to center and swivel **left** heel to center
5- 6	Swivet to left
	5 Swivel **left** toe to left and swivel **right** heel to right
	6 Swivel **left** toe to center and swivel **right** heel to center
7- 8	Swivet to left
	7 Swivel **left** toe to left and swivel **right** heel to right
	8 Swivel **left** toe to center and swivel **right** heel to center
9-10	Swivet to right
	9 Swivel **right** toe to right and swivel **left** heel to left
	10 Swivel **right** toe to center and swivel **left** heel to center
11-12	Swivet to right
	11 Swivel **right** toe to right and swivel **left** heel to left
	12 Swivel **right** toe to center and swivel **left** heel to center
13-14	Swivet to left
	13 Swivel **left** toe to left and swivel **right** heel to right
	14 Swivel **left** toe to center and swivel **right** heel to center
15-16	Swivet to right
	15 Swivel **right** toe to right and swivel **left** heel to left
	16 Swivel **right** toe to center and swivel **left** heel to center
	Touches and Turn
17	Touch **right** heel forward
18	Touch **right** toe back
19	Step **right** foot forward and pivot 1/4 turn right

20 Touch **left** toe to left side
21 Step **left** foot across **right** foot
22 Touch **right** toe to right side

Jazz Box with Jump

23-26 Right jazz box with jump
- 23 Step **right** foot across **left** foot
- 24 Step **left** foot back
- 25 Step **right** foot to right side
- 26 Jump forward

Repeat Pattern

Rhythm Line:

```
secs      .....1.....2.....3.....4.....5.....6.....7.....8.....9....10
120 bpm    1  2  3  4  1  2  3  4  1  2  3  4  1  2  3  4  1  2  3  4
foot       B  B  B  B  B  B  B  B  B  B  B  B  B  B  B  B  R  R  R  L

secs      ....11....12....13....14....15....16....17....18....19....20
120 bpm    1  2  3  4  1  2  3  4  1  2  3  4  1  2  3  4  1  2  3  4
foot       L  R  R  L  R  B  —Repeat Pattern—
```

Cues:

left / center / right / center
left / center / left / center
right / center / right / center
left / center / right / center
heel / toe
turn / touch / across / touch
across / back / side / jump

SWIVEL HEELS TO LEFT

SWIVEL TOES TO RIGHT

SWIVET TO RIGHT

HEEL AND TOE SWIVELS AND A SWIVET

THAT RESULT IN SIMILAR FOOT POSITIONS

Metamorphosized

About this dance: This dance was choreographed to go with the song "Bubba Hyde" by Diamond Rio. Once you've mastered the steps, listen to the lyrics as you dance. The style of the dance changes to match the metamorphosis of Barney Jekyll into Bubba Hyde. If the initial steps are done in a heavy, clumsy manner, "with a snap of the fingers", there is a sudden change in style on the sailor steps.

Note: the knee swivels, on beats 17-20, are easier to do if your right knee is slightly bent and you twist your foot in and out on the ball.

New Concepts, Steps and Combinations

New Combination

Monterey Turn

Instructs you to make a 1/2 turn in four beats of music. The direction of the turn will be specified in the dance description. On beat one, touch the lead foot (the foot in the direction of the turn) to the side. On beat two, on the ball of the following foot, pivot 1/2 turn in the direction specified. Step the lead foot next to the following foot as the turn is completed. On beat three, touch the toe of the following foot to the side. On beat four, step the following foot next to the lead foot.

For example, "Monterey turn to the right" instructs you to: on "1", touch your right toe to the side; on "2", pivot 1/2 turn to the right on your left foot, stepping your right foot next to your left as you complete this turn; on "3", touch your left toe to the left side; on "4", step your left foot next to your right.

The Dance

Difficulty Level: IV

Choreographer: James O. Kellerman

Dance Faces: four directions

Pattern Length: 32 Beats

Suggested Music:

For practicing – "Walkin' Away A Winner" by Kathy Mattea (Track 1 on your ***Free CD***).

For dancing – "Bubba Hyde" by Diamond Rio. "Givin' Water To A Drowning Man" by Lee Roy Parnell.

Beats	Description
	Stomps
1	Stomp **right** foot forward
2	Hold
3	Stomp **left** foot forward
4	Hold
5	Stomp **right** foot forward
6	Snap fingers
	Sailor Steps and Turn
7-8	Left sailor step (begin behind) with 1/8 turn right
	7 Step **left** foot behind **right** foot (leaning body slightly left)
	& Step **right** foot to right side and pivot 1/8 turn right
	8 Step **left** foot to left side
9-10	Right sailor step (begin behind) with 1/8 turn right
	9 Step **right** foot behind **left** foot (leaning body slightly right)
	& Step **left** foot to left side
	10 Step **right** foot to right side and pivot 1/8 turn right
11-12	Left sailor step (begin behind)
	11 Step **left** foot behind **right** foot (leaning body slightly left)
	& Step **right** foot to right side
	12 Step **left** foot to left side
	Twist, Turn, Kick-Ball-Change
13	Pivot on **both** feet 1/8 turn right
14	Pivot on **both** feet 3/8 turn left
15-16	Right kick-ball-change
	15 Kick **right** foot forward
	& Step ball of **right** foot next to **left** foot
	16 Step **left** foot in place

Knee Swivels and Hip Rolls

17 Touch **right** toe to right side and swivel **right** knee to right side
& Return **right** knee to center
18 Swivel **right** knee to right side
& Return **right** knee to center
19 Swivel **right** knee to right side
& Return **right** knee to center
20 Step **right** foot in place

21-22 Half hip roll, clockwise (begin right hip to right side)
23-24 Half hip roll, clockwise (begin right hip to right side)

Kicks and Turn

25 Kick **right** foot forward
26 Flick **right** foot and pivot on **left** foot 1/4 turn left
27 Stomp **right** foot in place
28 Stomp **left** foot in place

29-32 Right Monterey turn
- 29 Touch **right** toe to right side
- 30 Pivot on **left** foot 1/2 turn right and step **right** foot next to **left** foot (as turn is completed)
- 31 Touch **left** toe to left side
- 32 Step **left** foot next to **right** foot

Repeat Pattern

Rhythm Line:

```
secs     .....1.....2.....3.....4.....5.....6.....7.....8.....9....10
120 bpm   1  2  3  4  1  2  3 & 4 1 & 2 3 & 4  1  2  3 & 4 1 & 2 & 3 & 4
foot      R  .  L  .  R  .  L R L R L R L R L  B  B  R R L R R R R R R R
other                    fs                                kk kk kk
                   (Finger snap)                         (knee rolls)

secs     ....11....12....13....14....15....16....17....18....19....20
120 bpm   1  2  3  4  1  2  3  4  1  2  3  4  1  2  3  4  1  2  3& 4
foot     -B -  - B-   R  R  R  L  R  B  L  L  Repeat Pattern
other    -hip- -hip-
         (hip rolls)
```

Cues:

stomp / hold / stomp / hold
stomp / snap
behind-turn-side / behind -side-turn / behind-side-side
twist / twist / kick - ball - change
out-in-out-in-out-in-step
roll / roll / roll / roll
kick / turn / stomp / stomp
touch / turn / touch / step

Kickin' Ass

About this dance: This is not Judy's favorite dance because of all the jumping. When she dances it, she always replaces the jump-cross-turns with the variation. The movements on beats 9-11 and 13-15 of this pattern will take some practice as they involve weight changes so quick that they often look like jumps.

New Concepts, Steps and Combinations

New Combinations

Heel Click Instructs you to make two movements in one beat of music. On the half beat before "one", swivel your right heel to the right and left heel to the left. On beat one, swivel the heels to the center until they meet, usually with a sound. To accomplish the heel click, be sure to keep your body weight over the balls of the feet. A heel click is a double-time heel split.

Jump-Cross-Turn Instructs you to make two jumps and one turn in three beats of music. The direction of the turn will be specified in the dance description. On beat one, the dancer jumps, landing with both feet about shoulder width apart. On beat two, the dancer jumps again, landing with the legs crossed. The leg which is named by the direction of the turn must be crossed behind the other leg. On beat three, the dancer pivots ½ turn in the direction specified, "uncrossing" the legs. As with vines and many other three step combinations, a fourth, finishing move is often specified when a jump-cross-turn is used in 4/4 time music.

For example, "jump-cross-turn to the left" instructs you to: on "1", jump and land with feet apart; on "2", jump and land with left leg crossed behind right leg; on "3", pivot ½ turn to the left on the balls of both feet.

Some dancers find jump-cross-turns too jarring, especially when several are done in rapid succession. Consequently, an alternative to the jump-cross-turn has been developed. It proceeds as follows: on beat one, touch, to the side, the toe of the foot opposite the direction of the turn; on beat two, step the foot opposite the direction of the turn across the other foot (leaving weight on both feet); on beat three, pivot ½ turn in the direction specified (as in the jump-cross-turn).

For example, (replacing a jump-cross-turn to the left): on "1", touch your right toe to the right side; on "2", step your right foot across your left foot; on "3", pivot ½ turn to the left on the balls of both feet.

The Dance

Difficulty Level: IV

Choreographer: Unknown

Dance Faces: two directions

Pattern Length: 32 Beats

Suggested Music:

For practicing – "Talk Some" – originally recorded by Billy Ray Cyrus (Track 3 on your ***Free CD***).

For dancing – "The South's Gonna Do It" – originally recorded by Charlie Daniels Band (Track 6 on your ***Free CD***). "Dance" by Twister Alley.

Beats	Description
	Stomps and Clicks
1	Stomp **left** foot forward
2	Stomp **right** foot next to **left** foot
&3	Heel click & Swivel heels apart 3 Swivel heels to center
&4	Heel click & Swivel heels apart 4 Swivel heels to center
	Jump-cross-turn
5-8	Jump-cross-turn to the left with clap 5 Jump, landing with feet apart 6 Jump, landing with **right** foot across **left** foot 7 Pivot on **both** feet ½ turn left 8 Clap
	Heels and Claps
9	Touch **right** heel diagonally forward
10	Step **right** foot home and touch **left** heel diagonally forward
11	Step **left** foot home and touch **right** heel diagonally forward
12	Clap
13	Step **right** foot home and touch **left** heel diagonally forward
14	Step **left** foot home and touch **right** heel diagonally forward
15	Step **right** foot home and touch **left** heel diagonally forward
16	Clap
	Vines
17-20	Left vine with right touch 17 Step **left** foot to left side 18 Step **right** foot behind **left** foot 19 Step **left** foot to left side 20 Touch **right** foot next to **left** foot

21-24 Right vine with left kick

- 21 Step **right** foot to right side
- 22 Step **left** foot behind **right** foot
- 23 Step **right** foot to right side
- 24 Kick **left** foot forward

Steps and Kicks

25 Step **left** foot back
26 Step **right** foot back
27 Step **left** foot forward
28 Kick **right** foot forward

29 Step **right** foot back
30 Step **left** foot back
31 Step **right** foot forward
32 Kick **left** foot forward

Repeat Pattern

Variation

To avoid the jumping, some dancers replace steps 5 and 6 with:

5 Touch **right** foot to right side
6 Step **right** foot across **left** foot

Rhythm Line:

```
secs     .....1.....2.....3.....4.....5.....6.....7.....8.....9....10
180 bpm  1 2 3 4 1 2 3 4 1 2 3 4 1 2 3 4 1 2 3 4 1 2 3 4 1 2 3 4 1 2
foot     L R B B B B B . R L R . L R L . L R L R R L R L L R L R R L
other                  c       c       c

secs     ....11....12....13....14....15....16....17....18....19....20
180 bpm  3 4 1 2 3 4 1 2 3 4 1 2 3 4 1 2 3 4 1 2 3 4 1 2 3 4 1 2 3 4
foot     R L   Repeat Pattern
other
```

Cues:

stomp / stomp / and-click-and-click
apart / across / turn / clap
heel / heel / heel / clap
heel / heel / heel / clap
left / behind / left / touch
right / behind / right / kick
back / back / forward / kick
back / back / forward / kick

Trashy Women

About this dance: Pat's advice when teaching this dance is, "Look trashy." Although most men leave them out, women should remember to add the shoulder shimmies on beats 29-32 for a complete "trashy" look.

New Concepts, Steps and Combinations

New Concept

Lock Indicates a foot position in which one leg is crossed tightly over the other.

For example "Slide **left** foot back to lock across **right** foot" indicates that at the end of the slide, the left leg should be crossed over the right leg.

The Dance

Difficulty Level: IV

Choreographer: Pat Eodice

Dance Faces: two directions

Pattern Length: 56 Beats

Suggested Music:

For practicing – "I Wanna Go Too Far" – originally recorded by Trisha Yearwood (Track 4 on your ***Free CD***).

For dancing – "Shut Up And Kiss Me" – originally recorded by Mary Chapin Carpenter (Track 8 on your ***Free CD***). "Trashy Women" by Confederate Railroad.

Beats	**Description**
	Steps and Slides
1	Step **left** foot to left side
2	Slide **right** foot next to **left** foot
3	Step **left** foot to left side
4	Slide-up **right** foot next to **left** foot
5	Step **right** foot to right side
6	Slide **left** foot next to **right** foot
7	Step **right** foot to right side
8	Slide-up **left** foot next to **right** foot
	Turn
&	Step **left** foot to left side
9	Step **right** foot to right side
&	Step **left** foot home
10	Step **right** foot across **left** foot
11	Pivot on **both** feet $1/2$ turn to the left
12	Clap
	Hip Bumps and Rolls
13	Step **left** foot diagonally forward and bump **left** hip diagonally forward
14	Hold
15	Bump **right** hip diagonally back
16	Hold
17-18	Half hip roll, clockwise (begin right hip diagonally back)
19-20	Half hip roll, clockwise (begin right hip diagonally forward)
	Kicks
21	Kick **right** foot across **left** leg
22	Step **right** foot forward
23	Kick **left** foot across **right** leg
24	Step **left** foot forward

25	Kick **right** foot across **left** leg
26	Step **right** foot forward
27	Kick **left** foot across **right** leg
28	Step **left** foot across **right** foot
	Lock-Slide Back
&	Step **right** foot back (women also shimmy shoulders)
29	Slide **left** foot back to lock across **right** foot (women also shimmy shoulders, men clap)
&	Step **right** foot back (women also shimmy shoulders)
30	Slide **left** foot back to lock across **right** foot (women also shimmy shoulders, men clap)
&	Step **right** foot back (women also shimmy shoulders)
31	Slide **left** foot back to lock across **right** foot (women also shimmy shoulders, men clap)
&	Step **right** foot back (women also shimmy shoulders)
32	Slide **left** foot back to lock across **right** foot (women also shimmy shoulders, men clap)
	Turns
33-36	Right Monterey turn
	33 Touch **right** toe to right side
	34 Pivot on **left** foot ½ turn right and step **right** foot next to **left** foot (as turn is completed)
	35 Touch **left** toe to left side
	36 Step **left** foot next to **right** foot
37-40	Right Monterey turn
	37 Touch **right** toe to right side
	38 Pivot on **left** foot ½ turn right and step **right** foot next to **left** foot (as turn is completed)
	39 Touch **left** toe to left side
	40 Step **left** foot next to **right** foot
	Steps Back
41	Step **left** foot diagonally back
42	Touch **right** foot next to **left** foot and clap
43	Step **right** foot diagonally back
44	Touch **left** foot next to **right** foot and clap
45	Step **left** foot diagonally back
46	Touch **right** foot next to **left** foot and clap
47	Step **right** foot diagonally back
48	Touch **left** foot next to **right** foot and clap
	Hip Bumps** and **Rolls
49	Step **left** foot diagonally forward and bump **left** hip diagonally forward
50	Hold
51	Bump **right** hip diagonally back
52	Hold
53-54	Half hip roll, counter-clockwise (begin left hip diagonally forward)
55-56	Half hip roll, counter-clockwise (begin left hip diagonally forward)

Repeat Pattern

Rhythm Line:

```
secs     .....1.....2.....3.....4.....5.....6.....7.....8.....9....10
120 bpm    1  2  3  4  1  2  3  4&1&2  3  4  1  2  3  4  1  2  3  4
foot       L  R  L  R  R  L  R  LLRLR  .  L  .  .  .  .  .  .  .
other                                  c  b  b  b  b  roll  roll
                                     (clap) (bumps)  (hiprolls)

secs     ....11....12....13....14....15....16....17....18....19....20
120 bpm    1  2  3  4  1  2  3  4&1&2&3&4  1  2  3  4  1  2  3  4
foot       R  R  L  L  R  R  L  LRLRLRLRL  R  R  L  L  R  R  L  L
other                            c  c  c  c
                               (or shimmies)

secs     ....21....22....23....24....25....26....27....28....29....30
120 bpm    1  2  3  4  1  2  3  4  1  2  3  4  1  2  3  4  1  2  3  4
foot       L  R  R  L  L  R  R  L  L  .  .  .  .  .  .  .  L  L Repeat
other                              b  b  b  b  roll  roll
```

Cues:

left / slide / left / touch
right / slide / right / touch
left-right-home-across / turn / clap
bump / hold / bump / hold
roll / roll / roll / roll
kick / step / kick / step
kick / step / kick / across
back-lock-back-lock-back-lock-back-lock
touch / turn / touch / step
touch / turn / touch / step
back / touch / back / touch
back / touch / back / touch
bump / hold / bump / hold
roll / roll / roll / roll

CMT's Dance Ranch Romp

About this dance: This dance was choreographed by Jo Thompson for Country Music Television (CMT) as their signature dance. CMT has hosted several competitions at which Jo would teach the dance in a morning session, and dancers would compete in an afternoon session. This dance will introduce some tricky foot moves to you, including the *electric kick*. Try learning this dance real fast!

New Concepts, Steps and Combinations

New Step

Brush Hands The emphasis is not on the sound (there will be very little), but on the movement of the hands. The dance description will indicate which hand moves up and which moves down. One palm slides across the other with one hand moving up and the other hand moving down.

New Combinations

Heel Grind Instructs you to make two movements in one beat of music with the identified foot. On "1", with your foot turned in, step forward on your heel, the weight of your body placed on the heel. On "&", swivel your toe to the outside, keeping your weight on the heel.

For example, "right heel grind" instructs you to, on beat one, step forward on your right heel with foot turned in, and on "and", swivel your right toe from diagonally left to diagonally right.

Electric Kick Instructs you to make four movements in two beats of music. The foot which "kicks" will be identified in the dance description, while the other foot "supports" the weight during the kick. On the half beat before "1", the support foot steps diagonally back. On "1", the heel of the kicking foot touches diagonally forward. On "&", the kicking foot steps home. On "2", the support foot touches or steps next to the kicking foot, depending on the action required next. (Electric Kicks are also known as "Romps".)

For example, "left electric kick" instructs you to: on "&", step diagonally back on your right foot; on "1", touch your left heel diagonally forward; on "&", step your left foot home; and on "2", touch your right foot next to your left foot.

Most dancers find the electric kick very difficult to do at first. As with all dance steps, it gets easier with practice. Practice it very slowly and mechanically at first. Start by practicing small movements, and then try separating your feet more and more as you gain familiarity with the moves. As you become proficient with this combination, your four movements will begin to look like two, and your kicking leg will appear to be "flying" to its heel touch. Use caution when you first begin to practice this move. Judy has fallen learning the electric kick – then shot up like a rocket, powered by extreme embarrassment!

The Dance

Difficulty Level: IV

Choreographer: Jo Thompson

Dance Faces: four directions

Pattern Length: 48 Beats

Suggested Music:

For practicing – "Talk Some" – originally recorded by Billy Ray Cyrus (Track 3 on your ***Free CD***).

For dancing – "Redneck Girl" – originally recorded by Bellamy Brothers (Track 11 on your ***Free CD***). "Dance" by Twister Alley. "Stone Cold Country" by Gibson Miller Band.

Beats	Description
	Heel Grinds
1-&	Right heel grind
	1 Step **right** heel forward *(foot turned in)*
	& Swivel **right** toe to right
2	Step **left** foot in place
3	Step **right** foot slightly back
4	Step **left** foot in place
5-&	Right heel grind
	5 Step **right** heel forward *(foot turned in)*
	& Swivel **right** toe to right
6	Step **left** foot in place
7	Step **right** foot slightly back
8	Step **left** foot in place
	Turns and Stomps
9-10	Military turn to the left
	9 Step **right** foot forward
	10 Pivot on **both** feet ½ turn left
11-12	Military turn to the left
	11 Step **right** foot forward
	12 Pivot on **both** feet ½ turn left
13	Stomp **right** foot next to **left** foot
14	Stomp **left** foot next to **right** foot
15	Raise **both** toes slightly off the floor
16	Lower **both** toes to floor

Vines and Electric Kicks

17-20 Right vine with left touch
- 17 Step **right** foot to right side
- 18 Step **left** foot behind **right** foot
- 19 Step **right** foot to right side
- 20 Touch **left** foot next to **right** foot

21-22 Right electric kick
- & Step **left** foot diagonally back
- 21 Touch **right** heel diagonally forward
- & Step **right** foot home
- 22 Touch **left** foot home

23-24 Right electric kick
- & Step **left** foot diagonally back
- 23 Touch **right** heel diagonally forward
- & Step **right** foot home
- 24 Touch **left** foot home

25-28 Left vine with right touch
- 25 Step **left** foot to left side
- 26 Step **right** foot behind **left** foot
- 27 Step **left** foot to left side
- 28 Touch **right** foot next to **left** foot

29-30 Left electric kick
- & Step **right** foot diagonally back
- 29 Touch **left** heel diagonally forward
- & Step **left** foot home
- 30 Touch **right** foot home

31-32 Left electric kick
- & Step **right** foot diagonally back
- 31 Touch **left** heel diagonally forward
- & Step **left** foot home
- 32 Touch **right** foot home

Scoots and Turn

33 Step **right** foot forward
34 Scoot **right** foot forward and chug **left** leg
35 Step **left** foot back
36 Step **right** foot next to **left** foot

37 Step **left** foot forward
38 Scoot **left** foot forward and chug **right** leg
39 Step **right** foot back
40 Step **left** foot next to **right** foot

41 Step **right** foot forward
42 Scoot **right** foot forward and chug **left** leg
43 Step **left** foot across **right** foot
44 Step **right** foot back

Brush Hands

45	Step **left** foot to left side and pivot ¼ turn left
46	Stomp **right** foot next to **left** foot
47	Brush hands (move left hand down and right hand up)
48	Brush hands (move right hand down and left hand up)

Repeat Pattern

Rhythm Line:

```
secs      .....1.....2.....3.....4.....5.....6.....7.....8.....9....10
180 bpm    1&2 3 4 1&2 3 4 1 2 3 4 1 2 3 4 1 2 3 4&1&2&3&4 1 2 3 4&1&2
foot       RRL R L RRL R L R B R B R L B B R L R LLRRLLRRL L R L RRLLR
other

secs      ....11....12....13....14....15....16....17....18....19....20
180 bpm   &3&4 1 2 3 4 1 2 3 4 1 2 3 4 1&2 3 4 1&2 3 4 1 2 3 4 1 2 3 4
foot      RLLR R R L R L L R L L R . .  Repeat Pattern
other                                b b
                                (hand brushes)
```

Cues:

and-grind / left / back / left
and-grind / left / back / left
step / turn / step / turn
stomp / stomp / toes up / down
right / behind / right / touch
back-kick-and-home-back-kick-and-home
left / behind / left / touch
back-kick-and-home-back-kick-and-home
right / scoot / left / right
left / scoot / right / left
right / scoot / cross / turn
left / stomp / brush / brush

Wrong way to do an Electric Kick!

Kickin' Back

About this dance: It appears this dance takes its name from the movements like those at beats 15 and 16. Perhaps because of this, these movements are usually done with exceptional flourish. Dancers will notice that not only do the arm movements help to "show off" the move, they also help you keep your balance!

New Concepts, Steps and Combinations

New Combination

Lindy Instructs you to make a sideways shuffle and two rocks in four beats of music. The direction of movement will be specified in the dance description.

For example, "right Lindy" instructs you to: on "1&2", do a right shuffle to the right side; on "3", rock-step your left foot behind your right foot, as you face diagonally left; on "4", rock forward on your right foot, still facing diagonally left.

This combination produces a look of pulling away from a starting point and being "sprung" back to it. The shuffle and the first rock move smoothly in one direction. On the last rock, you will look as though you are being tugged back toward your starting point.

The Dance

Difficulty Level: IV

Choreographer: Scott Blevins

Dance Faces: four directions

Pattern Length: 48 Beats

Suggested Music:

For practicing – "Talk Some" – originally recorded by Billy Ray Cyrus (Track 3 on your ***Free CD***).

For dancing – "Baby Likes To Rock It" by The Tractors. "Good Brown Gravy" by Joe Diffy.

Beats	Description
	Walk Back with Claps
1	Step **right** foot diagonally back
2	Touch **left** foot next to **right** foot and clap
3	Step **left** foot diagonally back
4	Touch **right** foot next to **left** foot and clap

5	Step **right** foot diagonally back
6	Touch **left** foot next to **right** foot and clap
7	Step **left** foot diagonally back
8	Touch **right** foot next to **left** foot and clap

Side Steps, Swivets, and "Kick Backs"

9	Step **right** foot to right side
10	Slide **left** foot next to **right** foot
11	Step **right** foot to right side
12	Slide **left** foot next to **right** foot
13-14	Swivet to left
	13 Swivel **left** toe to left and swivel **right** heel to right
	14 Swivel **left** toe to center and swivel **right** heel to center
15	Raise **both** toes and raise both arms forward to chest height
16	Lower **both** toes and return arms to starting position
17	Step **left** foot to left side
18	Slide **right** foot next to **left** foot
19	Step **left** foot to left side
20	Slide **right** foot next to **left** foot
21-22	Swivet to right
	21 Swivel **right** toe to right and swivel **left** heel to left
	22 Swivel **right** toe to center and swivel **left** heel to center
23	Raise **both** toes and raise both arms forward to chest height
24	Lower **both** toes and return arms to starting position

Lindies

25-28	Right Lindy
	25 Step **right** foot to right side
	& Step **left** foot next to **right** foot
	26 Step **right** foot to right side
	27 Rock-step **left** foot behind **right** foot, face diagonally left
	28 Rock forward on **right** foot, face diagonally left
29-32	Left Lindy
	29 Step **left** foot to left side, face forward
	& Step **right** foot next to **left** foot
	30 Step **left** foot to left side
	31 Rock-step **right** behind **left** foot, face diagonally right
	32 Rock forward on **left** foot, face diagonally right

Rock Forward and Back

33	Rock-step **right** foot forward, face forward
34	Rock back on **left** foot
35	Rock-step **right** foot back
36	Rock forward on **left** foot

Military Turns

37-38 Military turn to the left
- 37 Step **right** foot forward
- 38 Pivot on **both** feet $\frac{1}{2}$ turn left

39-40 Military turn to the left
- 39 Step **right** foot forward
- 40 Pivot on **both** feet $\frac{1}{2}$ turn left

Jump and "Kick Back"

41 Jump forward
42 Clap
43 Raise **both** toes and raise both arms forward to chest height
44 Lower **both** toes and return arms to starting position

$\frac{1}{4}$ ***Turn and Kicks***

45 Pivot on heel of **left** foot and ball of **right** foot $\frac{1}{4}$ turn left
46 Stomp-up **right** foot next to **left** foot
47 Kick **right** foot forward
48 Kick **right** foot forward

Repeat Pattern

Rhythm Line:

```
secs     .....1.....2.....3.....4.....5.....6.....7.....8.....9....10
180 bpm  1 2 3 4 1 2 3 4 1 2 3 4 1 2 3 4 1 2 3 4 1 2 3 4 1&2 3 4 1&2
foot     R L L R R L L R R L R L B B B B L R L R B B B B RLR L R LRL
other      c   c   c   c
              (claps)

secs     ....11....12....13....14....15....16....17....18....19....20
180 bpm  3 4 1 2 3 4 1 2 3 4 1 2 3 4 1 2 3 4 1 2 3 4 1 2 3 4 1 2 3 4
foot     R L R L R L R B R B B . B B B R R R   Repeat Pattern
other                              c
                                 (clap)
```

Cues:

back / touch / back / touch
back / touch / back / touch
right / slide / right / slide
left / center / up / down
left / slide / left / slide
right / center / up / down
right-together-right / rock back / forward
left-together-left / rock back / forward
rock forward / back / back / forward
step / turn / step / turn
jump / clap / up / down
turn / stomp / kick / kick

Attitude

About this dance: This dance has won awards in several competitions. It is a good example of the recent wave of high energy Country and Western dances.

The Dance

Difficulty Level: IV

Choreographer: Rick & Deborah Bates

Dance Faces: four directions

Pattern Length: 56 Beats

Suggested Music:

For practicing – "I'm So Miserable Without You" – originally recorded by Billy Ray Cyrus (Track 7 on your ***Free CD***).

For dancing – "The South's Gonna Do It" – originally recorded by Charlie Daniels Band (Track 6 on your ***Free CD***). "Born in the Dark" by Doug Stone.

Beats	Description
	Back Toe Struts with Finger Snaps
	(finger snaps may be done with either hand)
1- 2	Right toe strut back with finger snap
	1 Touch **right** toe back
	2 Lower **right** heel (step **right** foot down) and snap fingers
3- 4	Left toe strut back with finger snap
	3 Touch **left** toe back
	4 Lower **left** heel (step **left** foot down) and snap fingers
5- 6	Right toe strut back with finger snap
	5 Touch **right** toe back
	6 Lower **right** heel (step **right** foot down) and snap fingers
7- 8	Left toe strut back with finger snap
	7 Touch **left** toe back
	8 Lower **left** heel (step **left** foot down) and snap fingers
	Forward Shuffles and Jump Turn
9-10	Right shuffle forward
	9 Step **right** foot forward
	& Step **left** foot next to **right** foot
	10 Step **right** foot forward

11-12 Left shuffle forward
- 11 Step **left** foot forward
- & Step **right** foot next to **left** foot
- 12 Step **left** foot forward

13-16 Jump-cross-turn to left with clap
- 13 Jump, landing with feet apart
- 14 Jump, landing with **right** foot across **left** foot
- 15 Pivot on **both** feet ½ turn left
- 16 Clap

Diagonal Step Slides with Arm Pulls

(For beats 17-20, face diagonally right and for beats 21-23, face diagonally left.)

17 Step **right** foot diagonally forward and extend both arms diagonally right
18 Slide **left** foot next to **right** foot and pull arms back to body
19 Step **right** foot diagonally forward and extend both arms diagonally right
20 Slide-up **left** foot next to **right** foot and pull arms back to body

21 Step **left** foot diagonally forward and extend both arms diagonally left
22 Slide **right** foot next to **left** foot and pull arms back to body
23 Step **left** foot diagonally forward and extend both arms diagonally left
24 Slide **right** foot next to **left** foot and pull arms back to body, face forward

Twists and Kicks

25 Pivot on **both** feet ¼ turn right
26 Pivot on **both** feet ½ turn left
27 Pivot on **both** feet ½ turn right
28 Pivot on **both** feet ½ turn left

29 Kick **right** foot forward
30 Kick **right** foot forward
31 Step **right** foot back
32 Touch **left** toe back

Touches and Kick-Ball-Changes

33 Step **left** foot forward
34 Touch **right** foot next to **left** foot

35-36 Right kick-ball-change
- 35 Kick **right** foot forward
- & Step ball of **right** foot next to **left** foot
- 36 Step **left** foot in place

37-38 Right kick-ball-change
- 37 Kick **right** foot forward
- & Step ball of **right** foot next to **left** foot
- 38 Step **left** foot in place

39 Step **right** foot forward
40 Touch **left** foot next to **right** foot

Right Military Turns

41-42 Military turn to the right
- 41 Step **left** foot forward
- 42 Pivot on **both** feet ½ turn right

43-44 Military turn to the right
- 43 Step **left** foot forward
- 44 Pivot on **both** feet ½ turn right

Rock and Shuffle Back

45 Rock-step **left** foot forward
46 Rock back on **right** foot

47-48 Left shuffle back with ½ turn left
- 47 Step **left** foot back
- & Step **right** foot next to **left** foot and pivot ¼ turn left
- 48 Step **left** foot to left side and pivot ¼ turn left

Jazz Box and Electric Kicks

49-52 Right jazz box
- 49 Step **right** foot across **left** foot
- 50 Step **left** foot back
- 51 Step **right** foot to right side
- 52 Step **left** foot next to **right** foot

53-54 Right electric kick
- & Step **left** foot diagonally back
- 53 Touch **right** heel diagonally forward
- & Step **right** foot home
- 54 Step **left** foot home

55-56 Left electric kick
- & Step **right** foot diagonally back
- 55 Touch **left** heel diagonally forward
- & Step **left** foot home
- 56 Step **right** foot home

Rhythm Line:

```
secs      .....1.....2.....3.....4.....5.....6.....7.....8.....9....10
180 bpm    1 2 3 4 1 2 3 4 1&2 3&4 1 2 3 4 1 2 3 4 1 2 3 4 1 2 3 4 1 2
foot       R R L L R R L L RLR LRL B B B . R L R L L R L R B B B B R R
other       fs  fs  fs  fs                 c

secs      ....11....12....13....14....15....16....17....18....19....20
180 bpm    3 4 1 2 3&4 1&2 3 4 1 2 3 4 1 2 3&4 1 2 3 4&1&2&3&4 1 2 3 4
foot       R L L R RRL RRL R L L B L B L R LRL R L R LLRRLRLLR  Repeat
other                                                           Pattern
```

Cues:

oe / heel / toe / heel
oe / heel / toe / heel
ight-together-right / left-together-left
ıpart / across / turn / clap
step / slide / step / slide
step / slide / step / slide
quarter / half / half / half
kick / kick / back / touch
step / touch / kick-ball-change
kick-ball-change / step / touch
step / turn / step / turn
ock forward / back / back-turn-turn
across / back / side / together
back-kick-and-home-back-kick-and-home

THE RIGHT "ATTITUDE"

Dances done in a circle

Introduction To The Dances

The dances in this section are designed to be done with dancers arranged in a circular pattern. Sometimes this arrangement is called "spoke line" to contrast it with "parallel or drill lines". To dance in spoke lines, a small number of dancers form a circle in the center of the floor, with lines of other dancers forming behind each of the people in the original circle. An aerial view would reveal a pattern that looked liked the hub and spokes of a big wheel. In this type of circle formation, dancers face the backs of other dancers. Unlike line dances, many circle dances progress around the dance floor. The progression of Country and Western circle dances is usually counter-clockwise. (We find it interesting that some American Indian circle dances progress clockwise, following the sun.)

Some circle dances are rather complicated. Instead of all dancers facing the center of the dance floor, circles alternate between facing the center and facing the outside of the dance floor. In this type of circle formation, dancers will be face to face with other dancers (at least until the music starts, and one circle goes counter-clockwise and the other goes clockwise).

Traveling Four Corners

About this dance: This dance may be done in concentric circles, with all dancers facing the center of the dance floor. Most often, however, dancers form concentric circles with alternate circles facing away from the center of the dance floor or toward the center of the dance floor so that dancers face each other. When Traveling Four Corners is done with dancers facing each other, on beats 1, 3, and 5, dancers clap hands with those facing them.

The Dance

Difficulty Level: I

Choreographer: Unknown

Circle Dance

Pattern Length: 20 Beats

Suggested Music:

For practicing – "I'm So Miserable Without You" – originally recorded by Billy Ray Cyrus (Track 7 on your ***Free CD***).

For dancing – "Dixie On My Mind" by Hank Williams, Jr.

Beats	Description
	Heel and Place
1	Touch **left** heel forward (Clap right hands with opposite dancer)
2	Step **left** foot next to **right** foot
3	Touch **right** heel forward (Clap left hands with opposite dancer)
4	Step **right** foot next to **left** foot
	Heel and Vine Left
5	Touch **left** heel forward (Clap right hands with opposite dancer)
6- 8	Left vine
	6 Step **left** foot to left side
	7 Step **right** foot behind **left** foot
	8 Step **left** foot to left side
	Heel and Vine Right
9	Touch **right** heel forward
10-12	Right vine
	10 Step **right** foot to right side
	11 Step **left** foot behind **right** foot
	12 Step **right** foot to right side

Turn and Vine Left

13 Hitch **left** leg and pivot on **right** foot ½ turn right

14-16 Left vine

- 14 Step **left** foot to left side
- 15 Step **right** foot behind **left** foot
- 16 Step **left** foot to left side

Turn and Vine Right

17 Hitch **right** leg and pivot on **left** foot ½ turn left

18-20 Right vine

- 18 Step **right** foot to right side
- 19 Step **left** foot behind **right** foot
- 20 Step **right** foot to right side

Repeat Pattern

Rhythm Line:

```
secs     .....1.....2.....3.....4.....5.....6.....7.....8.....9....10
120 bpm   1  2  3  4  1  2  3  4  1  2  3  4  1  2  3  4  1  2  3  4
foot      L  L  R  R  L  L  R  L  R  R  L  R  L  L  R  L  R  R  L  R
other     c     c     c
            (claps)
```

Cues:

heel / together / heel / together
heel / left / behind / left
heel / right / behind / right
turn / left / behind / left
turn / right / behind / right

The Rose

About this dance: This dance is well-named. It is done in concentric circles, and, if viewed from above, its pattern of forward and back movement would look like a flower opening and closing.

New Concepts, Steps and Combinations

New Combination

Toe Fan Instructs you to make two swivel movements of the identified foot in two beats of music. On "1", the toe swivels away from the stationary foot. On "2", the toe swivels to center.
For example, "right toe fan" instructs you, on beat one, to swivel your right toe to the right, and on beat two, to swivel your right toe to center.

The Dance

Difficulty Level: I

Choreographer: Unknown

Circle Dance

Pattern Length: 36 Beats

Suggested Music:

For practicing – "I'm So Miserable Without You" – originally recorded by Billy Ray Cyrus (Track 7 on your ***Free CD***).

For dancing – "I'm So Miserable Without You" – originally recorded by Billy Ray Cyrus (Track 7 on your ***Free CD***). "Friends In Low Places" by Garth Brooks.

Beats	Description
	Fans and Touches
1-2	Right toe fan 1 Swivel **right** toe to right 2 Swivel **right** toe to center
3-4	Right toe fan 3 Swivel **right** toe to right 4 Swivel **right** toe to center

5 Touch **right** heel forward
6 Touch **right** foot next to **left** foot
7 Touch **right** heel forward
8 Touch **right** foot next to **left** foot

Steps and Kicks

9 Step **right** foot forward
10 Step **left** foot forward
11 Kick **right** foot forward
12 Kick **right** foot forward

13 Step **right** foot back
14 Touch **left** foot next to **right** foot
15 Step **left** foot forward
16 Step **right** foot forward

17 Kick **left** foot forward
18 Kick **left** foot forward

Vine and Touches

19-22 Left vine diagonally back with right touch
- 19 Step **left** foot diagonally back
- 20 Step **right** foot behind **left** foot
- 21 Step **left** foot diagonally back
- 22 Touch **right** foot next to **left** foot

23 Step **right** foot to right side
24 Touch **left** foot behind **right** foot
25 Step **left** foot to left side
26 Touch **right** foot behind **left** foot

Vines with Turning Hitches

27-30 Right vine with left hitch and ½ turn right
- 27 Step **right** foot to right side
- 28 Step **left** foot behind **right** foot
- 29 Step **right** foot to right side
- 30 Hitch **left** leg and pivot on **right** foot ½ turn right

31-34 Left vine with right hitch and ½ turn left
- 31 Step **left** foot to left side
- 32 Step **right** foot behind **left** foot
- 33 Step **left** foot to left side
- 34 Hitch **right** leg and pivot on **left** foot ½ turn left

35 Stomp-up **right** foot next to **left** foot
36 Stomp-up **right** foot next to **left** foot

Repeat Pattern

Variation

On every other pattern repetition, on beats 5-8, military turns to the left are substituted for the heel touches, as follows:

5- 6	Military turn to the left	
	5	Step **right** foot forward
	6	Pivot on **both** feet ½ turn left
7- 8	Military turn to the left	
	7	Step **right** foot forward
	8	Pivot on **both** feet ½ turn left

Rhythm Line:

```
secs      .....1.....2.....3.....4.....5.....6.....7.....8.....9....10
120 bpm    1  2  3  4  1  2  3  4  1  2  3  4  1  2  3  4  1  2  3  4
foot       R  R  R  R  R  R  R  R  R  L  R  R  R  L  L  R  L  L  L  R

secs      ....11....12....13....14....15....16....17....18....19....20
120 bpm    1  2  3  4  1  2  3  4  1  2  3  4  1  2  3  4  1  2  3  4
foot       L  R  R  L  L  R  R  L  R  L  L  R  L  R  R  R  Repeat Pattern
```

Cues:

fan / home / fan / home
heel / touch / heel / touch
right / left / kick / kick
back / touch
left / right / kick / kick
back / behind / left / touch
right / touch / left / touch
right / behind / right / turn
left / behind / left / turn
stomp / stomp

Cherokee Kick

About this dance: This circle dance is sometimes done with dancers facing the center of the dance floor and sometimes with alternate circles facing away from the center. For extra styling, many dancers make small hops on the pivot leg as they do the hitch-turn moves (beats 22, 24, and 26). When danced in circles facing alternate directions, dancers often clap hands with the person opposite them on beats 8 and 12.

The Dance

Difficulty Level: II

Choreographer: Unknown

Circle dance

Pattern Length: 34 Beats

Suggested Music:

For practicing – "I'm So Miserable Without You" – originally recorded by Billy Ray Cyrus (Track 7 on your ***Free CD***).

For dancing – "Redneck Girl" – originally recorded by Bellamy Brothers (Track 11 on your ***Free CD***). "Cherokee Fiddle" by Johnny Lee.

Beats	Description
	Heel Swivels and Touches
1	Swivel heels to right
2	Swivel heels to center
3	Swivel heels to left
4	Swivel heels to center
5	Touch **right** heel forward
6	Touch **right** toe back
	Steps and Hitches
7	Step **right** foot forward
8	Hitch **left** leg and clap
9	Step **left** foot back
10	Touch **right** toe back
11	Step **right** foot forward
12	Hitch **left** leg and clap
13	Step **left** foot back
14	Touch **right** foot next to **left** foot

	Side and Touch
15	Step **right** foot to right side
16	Touch **left** foot next to **right** foot
17	Step **left** foot to left side
18	Touch **right** foot next to **left** foot
	Vine and Turns
19-22	Right vine with ½ turn right and left hitch
	19 Step **right** foot to right side
	20 Step **left** foot behind **right** foot
	21 Step **right** foot to right side
	22 Hitch **left** leg and pivot on **right** foot ½ turn right and clap
23	Step **left** foot to left side
24	Hitch **right** leg and pivot on **left** foot ½ turn right and clap
25	Step **right** foot to right side
26	Hitch **left** leg and pivot on **right** foot ¼ turn right and clap
	Steps and Scoots
27	Step **left** foot forward
28	Step **right** foot forward
29	Hitch **left** leg and scoot **right** foot forward and clap
30	Hitch **left** leg and scoot **right** foot forward and clap
31	Step **left** foot forward
32	Step **right** foot forward
33	Step **left** foot forward and pivot ¼ turn left
34	Stomp **right** foot next to **left** foot

Repeat Pattern

Rhythm Line:

secs		1		2		3		4		5		6		7		8		9		10
120 bpm	1	2	3	4	1	2	3	4	1	2	3	4	1	2	3	4	1	2	3	4
foot	B	B	B	B	R	R	R	L	L	R	R	L	L	R	R	L	L	R	R	L
other								c (clap)				c								

secs		11		12		13		14		15		16		17		18		19		20
120 bpm	1	2	3	4	1	2	3	4	1	2	3	4	1	2	3	4	1	2	3	4
foot	R	L	L	R	R	L	L	R	R	R	L	R	L	R	*Repeat Pattern*					
other				c		c			c	c										

Cues:

right / center / left / center
heel / toe
right / hitch / back / touch
right / hitch / back / together
right / touch / left / touch
right / behind / right / turn
left / turn / right / turn
left / right / scoot / scoot
left / right / turn / stomp

Dances done in contra lines

Introduction To The Dances

The dances in this section are designed to be done in contra lines. Contra lines are like drill lines in that dancers are arranged on the floor in sets of parallel lines. However, in drill line formation the dancers all face the same direction while in contra line formation dancers are arranged so that pairs of lines face each other. In other words, there are two lines of dancers across from each other. The most interesting feature of contra dances is that, on the appropriate beats, the dancers pass between one another, ultimately turning to again face one another. When you are doing a contra dance, whether in partnered or staggered lines, you should be about arm's length away from the line opposite you. This is generally referred to as "slapping distance" apart.

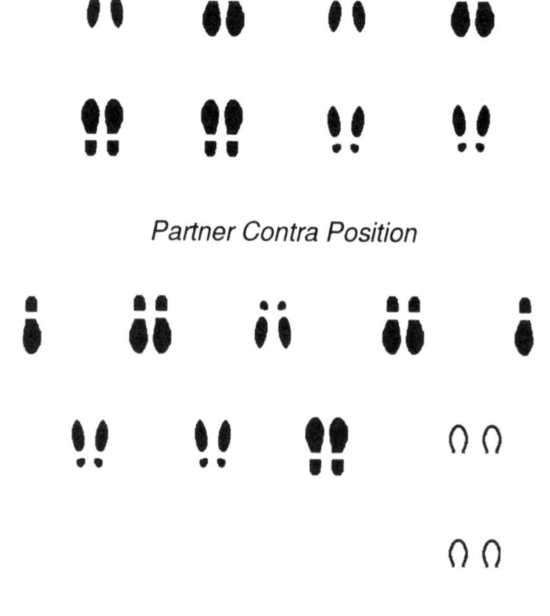

Partner Contra Position

Staggered Contra Position

Different types of Contra Dances

There are two different contra line formations: partner and staggered. The step description for each contra dance will indicate if dancers should be positioned opposite another dancer or a space. These formations are shown in the diagram. The upper set of footprints depicts dancers standing in "partner contra lines" or lines in which dancers are directly opposite one another. Some contra dances have dancers in one line standing opposite an empty space between the dancers in the other line, or in "staggered contra lines". The lower set of footprints depicts dancers in "staggered contra lines".

A word of **warning:** when you are first learning a contra dance, do not try to copy what the person across from you is doing, especially on the vines! You will end up going in the wrong direction with an inevitable crash. If you are unsure of your footwork, copy a person to the side of you.

Swingin' Gate

About this dance: This partnered contra dance, also known as Southside Shuffle, is most often done to fast music. When the floor is dancing Swingin' Gate, it is not uncommon for one person to run between the two lines which are facing each other, during the portion of the dance when dancers are not crossing from side to side. While we like Swingin' Gate and dance it often, neither one of us has ever tried to run between the lines. It seems too dangerous!

The step and stomps on beats 25-28 are used to realign the partners after they change lines.

These lines sure seem to get longer every year!

The Dance

Difficulty Level: II **Choreographer:** Unknown

Contra-Dance Faces: two directions **Pattern Length**: 28 Beats

Suggested Music:

For practicing – "The City Put The Country Back In Me" – originally recorded by Neal McCoy (Track 2 on your ***Free CD***).

For dancing – "The South's Gonna Do It" – originally recorded by Charlie Daniels Band (Track 6 on your ***Free CD***). "Born to Boogie" by Hank Williams, Jr.

Beats	Description
	Toe Fans
1- 2	Right toe fan
	1 Swivel **right** toe to right
	2 Swivel **right** toe to center
3- 4	Right toe fan
	3 Swivel **right** toe to right
	4 Swivel **right** toe to center
	Touches
5	Touch **right** heel forward
6	Touch **right** heel forward
7	Touch **right** toe back
8	Touch **right** toe back
9	Touch **right** heel forward
10	Touch **right** toe next to **left** foot
11	Touch **right** toe to right side
12	Touch **right** toe next to **left** foot
	Vines with Hitches and Claps
13-16	Right vine with left hitch
	13 Step **right** foot to right side
	14 Step **left** foot behind **right** foot
	15 Step **right** foot to right side
	16 Hitch **left** leg and clap
17-20	Left vine with right hitch and ¼ turn left
	17 Step **left** foot to left side
	18 Step **right** foot behind **left** foot
	19 Step **left** foot to left side
	20 Hitch **right** leg and pivot on **left** foot ¼ turn left and clap

Vine and Change Sides
(You should be ready to pass your partner back-to-back)

21-24 Right vine with left hitch and 3/4 turn right
- 21 Step **right** foot to right side
- 22 Step **left** foot behind **right** foot
- 23 Step **right** foot to right side
- 24 Hitch **left** leg and pivot on **right** foot 3/4 turn right

Steps and Stomps
(Use these four steps to align your position and distance)

25 Step **left** foot in place
26 Step **right** foot in place
27 Step **left** foot in place
28 Stomp-up **right** foot

Repeat Pattern

Variation

1. Some dancers replace the steps described for beats 5 -8 with military turns to the left.

2. Some dancers replace the vine on beats 13-15 with a three-step turn.

3. Some dancers replace the steps for beats 21-24 by linking right arms with the person across from them and making one full turn, returning to the "wall" they were on before the turn began.

Rhythm Line:

```
secs      .....1.....2.....3.....4.....5.....6.....7.....8.....9....10
180 bpm   1 2 3 4 1 2 3 4 1 2 3 4 1 2 3 4 1 2 3 4 1 2 3 4 1 2 3 4 1 2
foot      R R R R R R R R R R R R R L R L L R L R R L R L L R L R   Repeat
other                                     c       c                 Pattern
                                            (claps)
```

Cues:

fan / home / fan / home
heel / heel / toe / toe
heel / touch / side / touch
right / behind / right / hitch
left / behind / left / turn
right / behind / right / turn
left / right / left / stomp

Saturday Night Boogie

About this dance: This dance is done in staggered contra lines. On beat 4, the dancers pass between one another. As you pass, slap hands with the dancers on either side of you (left hand to the dancer on the left and right hand to the dancer on the right).

The Dance

Difficulty Level: II

Choreographer: Dale and Tanya Curry

Contra-Dance faces: two directions

Pattern Length: 36 Beats

Suggested Music:

For practicing – "The City Put The Country Back In Me" – originally recorded by Neal McCoy (Track 2 on your ***Free CD***).

For dancing – "The South's Gonna Do It" – originally recorded by Charlie Daniels Band (Track 6 on your ***Free CD***). "Felicia" by McBride and The Ride. "T-R-O-U-B-L-E" by Travis Tritt.

Beats	Description
	Step-Slides and Scuff-Turn
1	Step **right** foot forward
2	Slide **left** foot next to **right** foot
3	Step **right** foot forward
4	Scuff **left** foot and slap hands
5	Step **left** foot forward
6	Slide **right** foot next to **left** foot
7	Step **left** foot forward
8	Scuff **right** foot and pivot on **left** foot $1/4$ turn left
	Rocks and Scuff-Turns
9	Rock-step **right** foot forward
10	Rock back on **left** foot
11	Rock forward on **right** foot
12	Scuff **left** foot and pivot on **right** foot $1/2$ turn right
13	Rock-step **left** foot forward
14	Rock back on **right** foot
15	Rock forward on **left** foot
16	Scuff **right** foot and pivot on **left** foot $1/4$ turn left

17 Rock-step **right** foot forward
18 Rock back on **left** foot
19 Rock forward on **right** foot
20 Scuff **left** foot and pivot on **right** foot ½ turn right

21 Rock-step **left** foot forward
22 Rock back on **right** foot
23 Rock forward on **left** foot
24 Scuff **right** foot

Touches

25 Touch **right** heel forward
26 Touch **right** foot next to **left** foot
27 Touch **right** toe to right side
28 Touch **right** foot next to **left** foot

29 Step **right** foot to right side
30 Slide-up **left** foot next to **right** foot

31 Touch **left** heel forward
32 Touch **left** foot next to **right** foot
33 Touch **left** toe to left side
34 Touch **left** foot next to **right** foot

35 Step **left** foot to left side
36 Slide-up **right** foot next to **left** foot

Repeat Pattern

Rhythm Line:

```
secs      .....1.....2.....3.....4.....5.....6.....7.....8.....9....10
180 bpm    1 2 3 4 1 2 3 4 1 2 3 4 1 2 3 4 1 2 3 4 1 2 3 4 1 2 3 4 1 2
foot       R L R L L R L R R L R L L R L R R L R L L R L R R R R R R L
other            s
            (slap hands)

secs      ....11....12....13....14....15....16....17....18....19....20
180 bpm    3 4 1 2 3 4 1 2 3 4 1 2 3 4 1 2 3 4 1 2 3 4 1 2 3 4 1 2 3 4
foot       L L L L L R   Repeat Pattern
```

Cues:

right / slide / right / scuff
left / slide / left / turn
rock forward / back / forward / turn
rock forward / back / forward / turn
rock forward / back / forward / turn
rock forward / back / forward / scuff
heel / touch / side / touch
right / slide
heel / touch / side / touch
left / slide

Cotton-Eyed Joe (The Line Dance)

About this dance: This dance has "line dance" in its title to distinguish it from a very old partner dance which is also called Cotton-Eyed Joe. The line dance version was choreographed, as either a drill or contra dance, to match the updated version of the Cotton-Eyed Joe song by Rednex. We do Cotton-Eyed Joe (The Line Dance) in contra lines in which dancers are directly opposite each other. On beat 12, clap hands with the dancer opposite you.

New Concepts, Steps and Combinations

New Combinations

Coaster Step Instructs you to make three back and forward steps in two beats of music. The foot that leads the sequence will be identified in the dance description. On beat one, the lead foot steps back. On "and", the following foot steps next to the lead foot. On beat two, the lead foot steps forward. Because of the quick change of direction involved, the first two steps should be taken on the balls of the feet. This movement produces a look of the feet backing away from the body.

For example, "right coaster step" instructs you to: on "1", step back on the ball of your right foot, on "&", step the ball of your left foot next to your right, and on "2", step forward on your right foot.

Polka Instructs you to make a shuffle and one other movement in two and a half beats of music.The direction of the polka (forward, backward, or to the side) and the foot that begins, or leads, the polka will be specified in the dance description. The three shuffle steps take place on beats "1 & 2". The fourth step, which takes place on the next half-beat after beat "2", may be a kick, turn, or hop and will be specified in the dance description. The steps are done to a rhythm of "one-and-two-and".

For example, "right polka forward with ½ turn left" instructs you to: on "1", step forward on your right foot; on "&", step the ball of your left foot next to heel of your right foot; on "2", step forward on your right foot; on "&", pivot ½ turn left on the ball of your right foot.

The Dance

Difficulty Level: III **Choreographer:** Susan and Harry Brooks

Contra-Dance faces: two directions **Pattern Length**: 48 Beats

Suggested Music:

For practicing – "I Wanna Go Too Far" – originally recorded by Trisha Yearwood (Track 4 on your ***Free CD***).

For dancing – "Redneck Girl" – originally recorded by Bellamy Brothers (Track 11 on your ***Free CD***). "Cotton-Eyed Joe" by Rednex

---

Beats	Description
	Hooks and Shuffles
1	Hook **left** leg in front of **right** leg
2	Kick **left** foot forward
3-4	Left shuffle back
	3 Step **left** foot back
	& Step **right** foot next to **left** foot
	4 Step **left** foot back
5	Hook **right** leg in front of **left** leg
6	Kick **right** foot forward
7-8	Right shuffle back
	7 Step **right** foot back
	& Step **left** foot next to **right** foot
	8 Step **right** foot back
	Forward and Back with Coaster Step
9	Step **left** foot forward
10	Slide **right** foot next to **left** foot
11	Step **left** foot forward
12	Touch **right** toe next to **left** foot and clap
13	Step **right** foot back
14	Step **left** foot back
15-16	Right coaster step
	15 Step **right** foot back
	& Step **left** foot next to **right** foot
	16 Step **right** foot forward

Weaves, Touches and Stomps

17-20 Weave to the right (begin across)
- 17 Step **left** foot across **right** foot
- 18 Step **right** foot to right side
- 19 Step **left** foot behind **right** foot
- 20 Step **right** foot to right side

21 Touch **left** heel forward
22 Touch **left** toe to left side
23 Scuff **left** foot
& Hitch **left** leg
24 Stomp **left** foot next to **right** foot

25-28 Weave to the left (begin across)
- 25 Step **right** foot across **left** foot
- 26 Step **left** foot to left side
- 27 Step **right** foot behind **left** foot
- 28 Step **left** foot to **left** side

29 Touch **right** heel forward
30 Touch **right** toe to right side
31 Scuff **right** foot
& Hitch **right** leg
32 Stomp **right** foot next to **left** foot

Bumps

33 Step **left** foot diagonally forward and bump **left** hip diagonally forward
34 Bump **left** hip diagonally forward
35 Bump **right** hip diagonally back
36 Bump **right** hip diagonally back

37 Step **left** foot diagonally back and bump **left** hip diagonally back
38 Bump **left** hip diagonally back
39 Bump **right** hip diagonally forward
40 Bump **right** hip diagonally forward

Polkas With Turns

41-42 Left polka forward with ½ turn left
- 41 Step **left** foot forward
- & Step **right** foot next to **left** foot
- 42 Step **left** foot forward
- & Pivot on **left** foot ½ turn left

43-44 Right polka back with ½ turn left
- 43 Step **right** foot back
- & Step **left** foot next to **right** foot
- 44 Step **right** foot back
- & Pivot on **right** foot ½ turn left

45-46 Left polka forward with ½ turn left
- 45 Step **left** foot forward
- & Step **right** foot next to **left** foot
- 46 Step **left** foot forward
- & Pivot on **left** foot ½ turn left

47-48 Right shuffle in place
- 47 Step **right** foot in place
- & Step on ball of **left** foot next to **right**
- 48 Step **right** foot in place

Repeat Pattern

Variation

Some dancers replace the turning polkas on beats 41 to 44& with two shuffles forward.

Rhythm Line:

```
secs      .....1.....2.....3.....4.....5.....6.....7.....8.....9....10
120 bpm    1   2   3&4  1   2   3&4  1   2   3   4   1   2   3&4  1   2   3   4
foot       L   L   LRL  R   R   RLR  L   R   L   R   R   L   RLR  L   R   L   R
other

secs      ....11....12....13....14....15....16....17....18....19....20
120 bpm    1   2   3& 4  1   2   3   4   1   2   3&4  1   2   3   4   1   2   3   4
foot       L   L   LL L  R   L   R   L   R   R   RRR  L   .   .   .   L   .   .   .
other                                                 b   b   b   b   b   b   b   b
                                                            (hip bumps)

secs      ....21....22....23....24....25....26....27....28....29....30
120 bpm    1&2&3&4&1&2&3&4  1   2   3&4  1   2   3&4  1   2   3   4
foot       LR LL RL RR LR LL RL R   Repeat Pattern
other
```

Cues:

hook / kick / back-together-back
hook / kick / back-together-back
left / slide / left / touch
back / back / back-together-forward
across / right / behind / right
heel / toe / scuff-and-stomp
across / left / behind / left
heel / toe / scuff-and-stomp
bump / bump / bump / bump
bump / bump / bump / bump
left-together-left-turn-back-together-back-turn-
left-together-left-turn-right-left-right

Dances done to Country Cha Cha rhythms

Introduction to the Dances

The dances in this section are done to music played in Cha Cha rhythm. Cha Cha rhythms are 4/4 rhythms in that Cha Cha music has four beats per measure. However, unlike the music for the dances in the first section of this book in which beats 1, 2, 3, 4 are emphasized, country Cha Cha music emphasizes half beats between many of the full beats. This difference in music produces different patterns of dance steps. When we described the steps for 4/4 rhythm music, we presented them in clusters of four. In the Cha Chas, we will organize steps into clusters of five, with a step for each full beat, and a step for the half beat between three and four. This reflects the fact that country Cha Cha dancing is counted 1, 2, 3&4.

If you are familiar with another form of dancing, you may observe that you have counted Cha Cha dance steps differently in the past. (For example, ballroom dancers typically assign steps to beats 1, 2, 3, 4&.) This change in counting may feel awkward to you at first. Keep in mind that the country style is not wrong; it is simply different.

The Cha Chas included in this book are typically done in drill lines.

Stationary Cha Cha

About this dance: Some dancers do this as a partner dance. When they do, the pair of dancers uses one of the spaces in the drill line grid.

The Dance

Difficulty Level: II

Choreographer: Unknown

Dance Faces: four directions

Pattern Length: 28 Beats

Suggested Music:

For practicing – "Gulf Of Mexico" – originally recorded by Clint Black (Track 12 on your ***Free CD***).

For dancing – "Gulf Of Mexico" – originally recorded by Clint Black (Track 12 on your ***Free CD***). "Neon Moon" by Brooks and Dunn. "Oh What A Thrill" by The Mavericks.

Beats	**Description**
	Rock and Cha Cha
1	Rock-step **right** foot forward
2	Rock back on **left** foot
3-4	Right Cha Cha in place
	3 Step **right** foot next to **left** foot
	& Step **left** foot in place
	4 Step **right** foot in place
	Rock and Cha Cha With Turns
5	Rock-step **left** foot back
6	Rock forward on **right** foot
7-8	Left Cha Cha with ½ turn right
	7 Step **left** foot forward and pivot ¼ turn right
	& Step **right** foot in place and pivot ¼ turn right
	8 Step **left** foot next to **right** foot
9	Rock-step **right** foot back
10	Rock forward on **left** foot
11-12	Right Cha Cha with ½ turn left
	11 Step **right** foot forward and pivot ¼ turn left
	& Step **left** foot in place and pivot ¼ turn left
	12 Step **right** foot next to **left** foot

13 Rock-step **left** foot back
14 Rock forward on **right** foot

15-16 Left Cha Cha with $\frac{1}{4}$ turn right
- 15 Step **left** foot forward
- & Step **right** foot in place and pivot $\frac{1}{4}$ turn right
- 16 Step **left** foot next to **right** foot

Military Turn and Cha Cha

17-18 Military turn to the left
- 17 Step **right** foot forward
- 18 Pivot on **both** feet $\frac{1}{2}$ turn left

19-20 Right Cha Cha in place
- 19 Step **right** foot next to **left** foot
- & Step **left** foot in place
- 20 Step **right** foot in place

Military Turn, Rocks and Cha Cha

21-22 Military turn to the right
- 21 Step **left** foot forward
- 22 Pivot on **both** feet $\frac{1}{2}$ turn right

23 Rock-step **left** foot forward
24 Rock back on **right** foot
25 Rock forward on **left** foot
26 Rock back on **right** foot

27-28 Left Cha Cha in place
- 27 Step **left** foot next to **right** foot
- & Step **right** foot in place
- 28 Step **left** foot in place

Repeat Pattern

Rhythm Line:

```
secs      .....1.....2.....3.....4.....5.....6.....7.....8.....9....10
90 bpm       1   2   3 & 4   1   2   3 & 4   1   2   3 & 4   1   2   3
foot         R   L   R L R   L   R   L R L   R   L   R L R   L   R   L

secs      ....11....12....13....14....15....16....17....18....19....20
90 bpm     & 4   1   2   3 & 4   1   2   3   4   1   2   3 & 4   1   2
foot       R L   R   B   R L R   L   B   L   R   L   R   L R L Repeat Pattern
```

Cues:

rock forward / back / Cha-Cha-Cha
rock back / forward / turn - turn - Cha
rock back / forward / turn - turn - Cha
rock back / forward / Cha - turn - Cha
step / turn / Cha-Cha-Cha
step / turn / rock forward / back
rock forward / back / Cha-Cha-Cha

Tropical Depression

About this dance: The choreographer tells us he wanted a real Caribbean look to this dance. We think the hip sways and relatively subtle movements accomplish that. This dance is particularly fun when danced to "Tropical Depression" by Alan Jackson.

New Concepts, Steps and Combinations

New Step

Flare Instructs you to make a low kick, keeping the foot parallel to the floor. While a kick generally brings the foot about six inches off the floor, in a flare the foot is lifted only high enough to avoid touching the floor. The direction of the flare will be specified in the dance description.

New Combinations

Flare-Ball -Change Replaces the first move of a kick-ball-change with a flare forward. For example, "right flare-ball-change" instructs you to: on "1", flare your right foot forward (about one inch off the floor); on "&", step the ball of your right foot next to your left foot; on "2", step your left foot in place.

Touch-Ball -Change Replaces the first move of a kick-ball-change with a toe touch forward.
For example, "right touch-ball-change" instructs you to: on "1", touch your right toe forward; on "&", step the ball of your right foot next to your left foot; on "2", step your left foot in place.

The Dance

Difficulty Level: III

Dance Faces: four directions

Choreographer: Bill Ray

Pattern Length: 48 Beats

Suggested Music:

For practicing – "Gulf Of Mexico" – originally recorded by Clint Black (Track 12 on your ***Free CD***).

For dancing – "Gulf Of Mexico" – originally recorded by Clint Black (Track 12 on your ***Free CD***). "Tropical Depression" by Alan Jackson. "Mexican Minutes" by Brooks and Dunn.

Beats	Description
	Rock and Cha Cha
1	Rock-step **left** foot across **right** foot, face diagonally right
2	Rock back on **right** foot, face forward
3-4	Left Cha Cha in place
	3 Step **left** foot next to **right** foot
	& Step **right** foot in place
	4 Step **left** foot in place
5	Rock-step **right** foot across **left** foot, face diagonally left
6	Rock back on **left** foot, face forward
7-8	Right Cha Cha in place
	7 Step **right** foot next to **left** foot
	& Step **left** foot in place
	8 Step **right** foot in place
	Turn and Cha Cha
9-10	Military turn to the right
	9 Step **left** foot forward
	10 Pivot on both feet ½ turn right
11-12	Left Cha Cha in place
	11 Step **left** foot next to **right** foot
	& Step **right** foot in place
	12 Step **left** foot in place
13-14	Military turn to the left
	13 Step **right** foot forward
	14 Pivot on both feet ½ turn left
15-16	Right Cha Cha in place
	15 Step **right** foot next to **left** foot
	& Step **left** foot in place
	16 Step **right** foot in place
	Latin Side Step and Cha Cha
17	Latin-step **left** foot to left side
18	Latin-slide **right** foot next to **left** foot
19	Latin-step **left** foot to left side
20	Latin-slide **right** foot next to **left** foot

21	Rock-step **left** foot forward
22	Rock back on **right** foot
23-24	Left Cha Cha in place
	23 Step **left** foot next to **right** foot
	& Step **right** foot in place
	24 Step **left** foot in place
25	Latin-step **right** foot to right side
26	Latin-slide **left** foot next to **right** foot
27	Latin-step **right** foot to right side
28	Latin-slide **left** foot next to **right** foot
29	Rock-step **right** foot back
30	Rock forward on **left** foot
31-32	Right Cha Cha in place
	31 Step **right** foot next to **left** foot
	& Step **left** foot in place
	32 Step **right** foot in place
	Side Step and Touch-Ball-Change
33	Step **left** foot to left side
34	Touch **right** foot next to **left** foot
35-36	Right touch-ball-change
	35 Touch **right** toe forward
	& Step ball of **right** foot next to **left** foot
	36 Step **left** foot in place
37	Step **right** foot to right side
38	Touch **left** foot next to **right** foot
39-40	Left touch-ball-change
	39 Touch **left** toe forward
	& Step ball of **left** foot next to **right** foot
	40 Step **right** foot in place
	Latin Turn 3/4 Right.
	(On each of the following 8 steps, pivot slightly less than 1/8 turn.)
41	Latin-step **left** foot forward and pivot slightly right
42	Latin-step **right** foot in place and pivot slightly right
43	Latin-step **left** foot forward and pivot slightly right
44	Latin-step **right** foot in place and pivot slightly right
45	Latin-step **left** foot forward and pivot slightly right
46	Latin-step **right** foot in place and pivot slightly right
47	Latin-step **left** foot forward and pivot slightly right
48	Latin-step **right** foot in place and pivot slightly right

Repeat Pattern

Variation

1. Some dancers find the "touch-ball-changes" awkward to do and replace them with "flare-ball-changes" (i.e. low kick-ball-changes).

2. For the first 8 beats, the original choreography calls for more accentuated moves than those we presented. The original moves are as follows:

1	Rock-step **left** foot across **right** foot and pivot on **right** foot 1/4 turn right
2	Rock back on **right** foot
3-4	Left Cha Cha turning 1/4 turn left
	3 Step **left** foot back and pivot 1/8 turn left
	& Step **right** foot next to **left** foot
	4 Step **left** foot next to **right** foot and pivot 1/8 turn left
5	Rock-step **right** foot across **left** foot and pivot on **left** foot 1/4 turn left
6	Rock back on **left** foot
7-8	Right Cha Cha turning 1/4 turn right
	7 Step **right** foot back and pivot 1/8 turn right
	& Step **left** foot next to **right** foot
	8 Step **right** foot next to **left** foot and pivot 1/8 turn right

Rhythm Line:

```
secs     .....1.....2.....3.....4.....5.....6.....7.....8.....9....10
90 bpm      1    2    3 & 4    1    2    3 & 4    1    2    3 & 4    1    2    3
foot        L    R    L R L    R    L    R L R    L    B    L R L    R    B    R

secs     ....11....12....13....14....15....16....17....18....19....20
90 bpm    & 4    1    2    3    4    1    2    3 & 4    1    2    3    4    1    2
foot      L R    L    R    L    R    L    R    L R L    R    L    R    L    R    L

secs     ....21....22....23....24....25....26....27....28....29....30
90 bpm      3 & 4    1    2    3 & 4    1    2    3 & 4    1    2    3    4    1
foot        R L R    L    R    R R L    R    L    L L R    L    R    L    R    L

secs     ....31....32....33....34....35....36....37....38....39....40
90 bpm      2    3    4    1    2    3 & 4    1    2    3 & 4    1    2    3 & 4
foot        R    L    R    Repeat Pattern
```

Cues:

rock across / back / Cha Cha Cha
rock across / back / Cha Cha Cha
step / turn / Cha Cha Cha
step / turn / Cha Cha Cha
left / slide / left / slide
rock forward / back / Cha Cha Cha
right / slide / right / slide
rock back / forward / Cha Cha Cha
left / touch / touch-ball-change
right / touch / touch-ball-change
turn / turn / turn / turn
turn / turn / turn / turn

Sugar Kisses

About this dance: This is a new Cha Cha, but one that appears to be attracting the attention of many. One reason for this may be the fact that it incorporates many movements unique among line dance Cha Chas.

New Concepts, Steps and Combinations

New Combination

Rondé Instructs you to move the designated foot in an arc. The amount of movement (1/4 or 1/2 circle), the beginning position, and the beats in which the movement must be completed, will be specified in the dance description. The moving foot is either on the floor or raised slightly above it. The rondé is generally easier to execute if the knee of the leg supporting your weight is bent slightly. (Rondé is also known as rond de jambe.)

For example, "right 1/4 rondé (begin forward)" instructs you to touch your right toe forward and, leaving your leg extended, draw a quarter circle with your right toe, ending at the right side position.

The Dance

Difficulty Level: III

Choreographer: Connie Frendt

Dance Faces: four directions

Pattern Length: 32 Beats

Suggested Music:

For practicing – "Gulf Of Mexico" – originally recorded by Clint Black (Track 12 on your ***Free CD***).

For dancing – "Gulf Of Mexico" – originally recorded by Clint Black (Track 12 on your ***Free CD***). "Day Off" by Ronnie McDowell.

Beats	Description
	Rondés and Cha Chas
1-2	Right 1/4 rondé (begin forward)
3-4	Right Cha Cha in place
	3 Step **right** foot next to **left** foot
	& Step **left** foot in place
	4 Step **right** foot in place

5-6	Left ¼ rondé (begin forward)
7-8	Left Cha Cha in place
	7 Step **left** foot next to **right** foot
	& Step **right** foot in place
	8 Step **left** foot in place
	Hip Bumps
9	Step **right** foot diagonally back and bump right hip diagonally back
10	Bump right hip diagonally back
11	Step **left** foot diagonally back and bump left hip diagonally back
12	Bump left hip diagonally back
	Rocks
13	Rock-step **right** foot back
14	Rock forward on **left** foot
15	Rock-step **right** foot forward
16	Rock back on **left** foot
17	Rock-step **right** foot back
18	Rock forward on **left** foot
19	Rock-step **right** foot forward
20	Rock back on **left** foot
	Kicks, Turns, and Cha Chas
21	Kick **right** foot forward
22	Kick **right** foot forward and pivot on **left** foot ¼ turn right
23-24	Right Cha Cha in place
	23 Step **right** foot next to **left** foot
	& Step **left** foot in place
	24 Step **right** foot in place
25	Kick **left** foot forward
26	Kick **left** foot forward and pivot on **right** foot ¼ turn left
27-28	Left Cha Cha in place
	27 Step **left** foot next to **right** foot
	& Step **right** foot in place
	28 Step **left** foot in place
	Turn and Stomp
29	Step **right** foot forward
30	Pivot on both feet ¼ turn left
31	Stomp **right** foot next to **left** foot
32	Stomp **left** foot in place

Repeat Pattern

Rhythm Line:

```
secs      .....1.....2.....3.....4.....5.....6.....7.....8.....9....10
90 bpm       1   2   3 & 4   1   2   3 & 4   1   2   3   4   1   2   3
foot         R - R   R L R   L - L   L R L   R   .   L   .   R   L   R
other      (rondé)        (rondé)          b   b   b   b
                                             (hip bumps)

secs      ....11....12....13....14....15....16....17....18....19....20
90 bpm       4   1   2   3   4   1   2   3 & 4   1   2   3 & 4   1   2
foot         L   R   L   R   L   R   R   R L R   L   L   L R L   R   B
other

secs      ....21....22....23....24....25....26....27....28....29....30
90 bpm       3   4   1   2   3 & 4   1   2   3 & 4   1   2   3   4   1
foot         R   L   Repeat Pattern
other
```

Cues:

ron / dé / Cha-Cha-Cha
ron / dé / Cha-Cha-Cha
bump / bump / bump / bump
rock back / forward / forward / back
rock back / forward / forward / back
kick / turn / Cha-Cha-Cha
kick / turn / Cha-Cha-Cha
right / turn / stomp / stomp

Dances done to Waltz rhythms

Introduction to the Dances

The dances in this section are done to music played in waltz (3/4) rhythm. Waltz music is counted 1-2-3, 1-2-3 with a stress on the "1". Waltz dance steps are traditionally counted in two groups of three beats (1-2-3, 4-5-6). With some exceptions, your feet will alternate left-right-left, right-left-right, making it easy to remember which foot moves next: the one different from the one you just moved! When your feet deviate from this pattern, you are said to be dancing a syncopated pattern. We will alert you to this when it happens – in "Midnight Waltz".

In dancing a waltz, it is important to remember that these dances are distinguished not only by the type of music to which the dance is done, but by the style with which the steps are taken. Waltzing is characterized by a subtle accent or emphasis placed on the steps to the first beat of each three beat sequence. In waltz units that involve steps forward, back, or to the side, the accent involves a "fall" on the first beat, followed by a "rise" on beats two and three. The look of falling and rising is achieved by making the first step in each three step unit relatively long, while the second and third steps in each three step unit are relatively short.

The waltzes included in this book are typically done in drill lines. When other line dance styles are options, those are noted in the dance descriptions.

Butterfly Waltz

About this dance: Peggy was living in Mariposa, California when she wrote this dance. Since butterfly motifs abound in Mariposa ("butterfly", in Spanish), it seemed only natural to call this dance the "Butterfly Waltz". This dance is most often done in parallel lines, but in some places, it is done in a circle. When danced in a circle, all dancers begin facing the center of the dance floor (and flutter toward and away from an imaginary flower in the center).

Remember: in a waltz, the first of every three steps is accented.

The Dance

Difficulty Level: I

Choreographer: Peggy Cole

Dance Faces: two directions

Pattern Length: 30 Beats

Suggested Music:

For practicing – "(You Got Me Over) A Heartache Tonight" – originally recorded by Dolly Parton (Track 10 on your ***Free CD***).

For dancing – "(You Got Me Over) A Heartache Tonight" – originally recorded by Dolly Parton (Track 10 on your ***Free CD***). "I See It Now" by Tracy Lawrence.

Beats	Description
	Full Turn
1	Step **left** foot forward
2	Step **right** foot forward and pivot ½ turn left
3	Step **left** foot back
4	Step **right** foot back
5	Step **left** foot back and pivot ½ turn left
6	Step **right** foot forward
	Forward and Back
7	Step **left** foot forward
8	Step **right** foot forward
9	Step **left** foot forward

10	Step **right** foot back
11	Step **left** foot back
12	Step **right** foot next to **left** foot
	Cross Steps
13	Step **left** foot across **right** foot, face diagonally right
14	Step **right** foot to right side, face forward
15	Step **left** foot next to **right** foot
16	Step **right** foot across **left** foot, face diagonally left
17	Step **left** foot to left side, face forward
18	Step **right** foot next to **left** foot
	Forward and Back
19	Step **left** foot forward
20	Step **right** foot forward
21	Step **left** foot forward
22	Step **right** foot back
23	Step **left** foot back
24	Step **right** foot next to **left** foot
	½ ***Turn***
25	Step **left** foot forward
26	Step **right** foot forward and pivot ½ turn left
27	Step **left** foot back
28	Step **right** foot back
29	Step **left** foot back
30	Step **right** foot next to **left** foot

Repeat Pattern

Rhythm Line:

```
secs     .....1.....2.....3.....4.....5.....6.....7.....8.....9....10
90 bpm     1   2   3   1   2   3   1   2   3   1   2   3   1   2   3
foot       L   R   L   R   L   R   L   R   L   R   L   R   L   R   L

secs     ....11....12....13....14....15....16....17....18....19....20
90 bpm     1   2   3   1   2   3   1   2   3   1   2   3   1   2   3
foot       R   L   R   L   R   L   R   L   R   L   R   L   R   L   R
```

Cues:

left / turn / back
right / turn / forward
left / right / left
back / back / together
across / right / together
across / left / together
left / right / left
back / back / together
left / turn / back
back / back / together

Waltz Across Texas

About this dance: This waltz becomes a favorite of many who learn it. It is one of a few line dances that easily translate to a partner line-dance, so it is very good at getting everyone out on the floor. It is common to see both couples and individuals intermixed on the dance floor.

Remember to accent the first of each three steps.

The Dance

Difficulty Level: III

Choreographer: Lois and John Nielson

Dance Faces: one direction

Pattern Length: 48 Beats

Suggested Music:

For practicing – "(You Got Me Over) A Heartache Tonight" – originally recorded by Dolly Parton (Track 10 on your ***Free CD***).

For dancing – "I'd Rather Miss You" by Little Texas. "You Look So Good In Love" by George Strait. "Could I Have This Dance" by Anne Murray.

Beats	Description
	Cross Steps
1	Step **left** foot across **right** foot, face diagonally right
2	Step **right** foot to right side, face forward
3	Step **left** foot next to **right** foot
4	Step **right** foot across **left** foot, face diagonally left
5	Step **left** foot to left side, face forward
6	Step **right** foot next to **left** foot
	Forward and Back
7	Step **left** foot forward
8	Step **right** foot forward
9	Step **left** foot next to **right** foot
10	Step **right** foot forward
11	Step **left** foot forward
12	Step **right** foot next to **left** foot
13	Step **left** foot back
14	Step **right** foot back
15	Step **left** foot next to **right** foot

16 Step **right** foot back
17 Step **left** foot back
18 Step **right** foot next to **left** foot

Turn, Weave, and Rock to the Left

19-21 Three-step turn to the left
- 19 Step **left** foot to left side and pivot $\frac{1}{2}$ turn left
- 20 Step **right** foot to right side and pivot $\frac{1}{2}$ turn left
- 21 Step **left** foot to left side

22-24 Weave to the left (begin across)
- 22 Step **right** foot across **left** foot
- 23 Step **left** foot to left side
- 24 Step **right** foot behind **left** foot

25 Rock-step **left** foot to left side
26 Rock to right on **right** foot
27 Rock to left on **left** foot

Turn, Weave, and Rock to the Right

28-30 Three-step turn to the right
- 28 Step **right** foot to right side and pivot $\frac{1}{2}$ turn right
- 29 Step **left** foot to left side and pivot $\frac{1}{2}$ turn right
- 30 Step **right** foot to right side

31-33 Weave to the right (begin across)
- 31 Step **left** foot across **right** foot
- 32 Step **right** foot to right side
- 33 Step **left** foot behind **right** foot

34 Rock-step **right** foot to right side
35 Rock to left on **left** foot
36 Rock to right on **right** foot

Forward and Back with Turns

37 Step **left** foot forward
38 Step **right** foot forward and pivot $\frac{1}{2}$ turn left
39 Step **left** foot back

40 Step **right** foot back
41 Step **left** foot back
42 Step **right** foot next to **left** foot

43 Step **left** foot forward
44 Step **right** foot forward and pivot $\frac{1}{2}$ turn left
45 Step **left** foot back

46 Step **right** foot back
47 Step **left** foot back
48 Step **right** foot next to **left** foot

Repeat Pattern

Rhythm Line:

```
secs      .....1.....2.....3.....4.....5.....6.....7.....8.....9....10
90 bpm       1   2   3   1   2   3   1   2   3   1   2   3   1   2   3
foot         L   R   L   R   L   R   L   R   L   R   L   R   L   R   L

secs      ....11....12....13....14....15....16....17....18....19....20
90 bpm       1   2   3   1   2   3   1   2   3   1   2   3   1   2   3
foot         R   L   R   L   R   L   R   L   R   L   R   L   R   L   R

secs      ....21....22....23....24....25....26....27....28....29....30
90 bpm       1   2   3   1   2   3   1   2   3   1   2   3   1   2   3
foot         L   R   L   R   L   R   L   R   L   R   L   R   L   R   L

secs      ....31....32....33....34....35....36....37....38....39....40
90 bpm       1   2   3   1   2   3   1   2   3   1   2   3   1   2   3
foot         R   L   R   Repeat Pattern
```

Cues:

across / side / together
across / side / together
left / right / together
right / left / together
back / back / together
back / back / together
turn / turn / side
across / left / behind
rock / rock / rock
turn / turn / side
across / right / behind
rock / rock / rock
left / turn / back
back / back / together
left / turn / back
back / back / together

Midnight Waltz

About this dance: Why the title? Jo Thompson tells us she was visiting her parents in Texas and came up with these steps while dancing around the kitchen – and it was midnight! Midnight Waltz has some unusual syncopated moves for a waltz line dance. We think the draws and slow flares provide interesting breaks in the traditional waltz pattern.

Remember: in a waltz, the first of every three steps is accented.

New Concepts, Steps and Combinations

New Concept

Syncopated pattern Indicates a set of steps that deviate from the standard step pattern for a particular type of dance. For example, the standard step pattern for a waltz consists of three steps, either left-right-left or right-left-right. In a waltz, a set of steps like "step left, brush right, hitch right" (left-right-right) would represent a deviation from the standard and would be called "syncopated".

New Step

Lunge Instructs you to take a long step in the indicated direction, bending the knee of the stepping leg. When the step is forward, the move is like a fencing lunge.

Right Flare Forward

Right Kick Forward

RIGHT LEG POSITIONS FOR FLARE AND KICK

The Dance

Difficulty Level: III

Choreographer: Jo Thompson

Dance Faces: four directions

Pattern Length: 48 Beats

Suggested Music:

For practicing – "(You Got Me Over) A Heartache Tonight" – originally recorded by Dolly Parton (Track 10 on your ***Free CD***).

For dancing – "Their Hearts Were Dancing" by the Forrester Sisters. "Someone Must Feel Like A Fool Tonight" by Kenny Rogers.

Beats	Description
	Cross Steps with ½ Turns
1	Step **left** foot across **right** foot
2	Step **right** foot to right side, face diagonally left
3	Step **left** foot next to **right** foot, face diagonally left
4	Step **right** foot across **left** foot, face forward
5	Step **left** foot to left side and pivot ½ turn right
6	Step **right** foot next to **left** foot
7	Step **left** foot across **right** foot
8	Step **right** foot to right side, face diagonally left
9	Step **left** foot next to **right** foot, face diagonally left
10	Step **right** foot across **left** foot, face forward
11	Step **left** foot to left side and pivot ½ turn right
12	Step **right** foot next to **left** foot
	Lunges
13	Lunge **left** foot across **right** foot
14	Step **right** foot to right side
15	Step **left** foot next to **right** foot
16	Lunge **right** foot across **left** foot
17	Step **left** foot to left side
18	Step **right** foot next to **left** foot
	Cross Step and Weave
19	Step **left** foot across **right** foot
20	Step **right** foot to right side
21	Step **left** foot next to **right** foot
22-24	Weave to left (begin across) 22 Step **right** foot across **left** foot 23 Step **left** foot to left side 24 Step **right** foot behind **left** foot

	Steps and Draws
25	Step **left** foot to left side
26-27	Draw-up **right** foot next to **left** foot
28	Step **right** foot to right side
29-30	Draw-up **left** foot next to **right** foot
	Slow Flares and Turns
31	Step **left** foot forward
32-33	Slow flare **right** foot forward
34	Step **right** foot back
35	Step **left** foot back and pivot 1/2 turn left
36	Step **right** foot next to **left** foot
37	Step **left** foot forward
38-39	Slow flare **right** foot forward
40	Step **right** foot back
41	Step **left** foot back and pivot 1/2 turn left
42	Step **right** foot next to **left** foot
	1/4 ***Turn***
43	Step **left** foot forward and pivot 1/4 turn left
44	Step **right** foot next to **left** foot
45	Step **left** foot in place
46	Step **right** foot back
47	Step **left** foot next to **right** foot
48	Step **right** foot in place

Repeat Pattern

Variation

Two different variations are substituted for the slow flares (beats 32-33 and 38-39).

1. The choreographer, Jo Thompson, suggests the following: over the two beats, bend the knee of your right leg, raising your foot (toe pointed down) about half-way up the calf. Continuing this move, extend your right foot (toe pointed forward). The first part of this movement is called developpé.

2. The second variation follows more traditional Country and Western moves. On the first beat, brush your right foot forward and, on the second beat, hitch your right leg. The movements are opposite those in the first variation – more like undeveloppé!

Rhythm Line:

```
secs      .....1.....2.....3.....4.....5.....6.....7.....8.....9....10
90 bpm       1   2   3   1   2   3   1   2   3   1   2   3   1   2   3
foot         L   R   L   R   L   R   L   R   L   R   L   R   L   R   L

secs      ....11....12....13....14....15....16....17....18....19....20
90 bpm       1   2   3   1   2   3   1   2   3   1   2   3   1   2   3
foot         R   L   R   L   R   L   R   L   R   L   R   .   R   L   .

secs      ....21....22....23....24....25....26....27....28....29....30
90 bpm       1   2   3   1   2   3   1   2   3   1   2   3   1   2   3
foot         L   R   R   R   L   R   L   R   R   R   L   R   L   R   L

secs      ....31....32....33....34....35....36....37....38....39....40
90 bpm       1   2   3   1   2   3   1   2   3   1   2   3   1   2   3
foot         R   L   R   Repeat Pattern
```

Cues:

across / side / together
across / turn / together
across / side / together
across / turn / together
lunge / side / together
lunge / side / together
across / side / together
across / side / behind
left / draw / draw
right / draw / draw
left / slow / flare
back / turn / together
left / slow / flare
back / turn / together
turn / right / together
back / left / together

Our Concluding Thoughts

We hope this book has helped you learn line dancing in an easy and enjoyable way. The challenge is not over. There will always be new line dances to learn. If you have not already done so, you might also want to explore the world of partner pattern, or partner freestyle dancing. Just make sure you get out and dance!

We attempted to contact all of the known choreographers of the dances included in this book. Everyone we talked to was very helpful and we appreciate their interest in our book. To them, and to the choreographers we were not able to reach (known and unknown): thank you for creating these wonderful dances!

We are struck by the fact that this book appears in print 10 years (almost to the day!) of Tony's "I don't dance" proclamation. It makes you believe anything can happen.

Glossary

A

Alternating Knee Pops

Instructs you to sequentially flex and straighten the knees, alternating left and right, for the designated number of beats. The knee that flexes first (lead knee) will be specified in the instruction. On beat one, bend the lead knee by lifting the heel of that foot off the floor. On beat two, bend the following knee (by lifting its heel off the floor) and straighten the lead knee (by lowering its heel). On beat three, bend the lead knee and straighten the following knee. Continue this sequence of movements for the designated number of beats. Note that at the end of this sequence one of the heels will remain lifted off the floor.

For example, "for beats 1- 4 Alternating knee pops (begin left)" instructs you to:
On "1", bend left knee (raise left heel); on "2", bend right knee (raise right heel) and straighten left knee (lower left heel); on "3", bend left knee (raise left heel) and straighten right knee (lower right heel); on "4", bend right knee (raise right heel) and straighten left knee (lower left heel).

B

Boot hook combination

Instructs you to make a sequence of four movements, one of which will be a hook, in four beats of music. The four movements are executed by the identified leg, while the other leg supports the weight of the body. On beat one, the heel will touch diagonally forward, with foot turned out. On beat two, the foot is hooked in front of the weighted leg. On beat three, the heel is touched diagonally forward, with foot turned out. On beat four, the foot steps next to the weighted foot.

For example, "left boot hook combination" instructs you to: on "1", touch your left heel, with foot turned out, diagonally forward; on "2", hook your left leg in front of your right leg; on "3", touch your left heel, with foot turned out, diagonally forward; on "4", step your left foot next to your right.

Brush

Instructs you to move the specified foot by gently sliding the ball of the foot across the floor. Brushes are most often done forward, but the direction will be specified in the dance description. This movement is much like a "scuff", except that in a "scuff" the heel comes in contact with the floor (and makes considerable noise) whereas in a "brush", the ball of the foot is in contact with the floor (and produces much less noise). The brush involves no weight transfer.

For example, "brush **left** foot forward" instructs you to gently slide the ball of the left foot forward across the floor. In "brush **left** foot forward" the right foot supports your weight during and after the brush.

Brush Hands Instructs you to slide one palm across the other with one hand moving up and the other hand moving down. The emphasis is not on the sound (there will be very little), but on the movement of the hands. The dance description will indicate which hand moves up and which moves down.

Bump Gives you an instruction for hip movement independent of foot movement. Bump instructs you to move your hips, once, on the designated musical beat. The hip that moves out (right or left) and the direction of the bump (e.g. forward, backward) will be specified in the dance description. In a bump, your weight is supported by both feet. Bumps generally are easier to execute if the knees are bent slightly.

For example, "bump **right** hip to the right" instructs you to move your right hip to the right on the beat of music.

C

Cha Cha Instructs you to take three small steps to two beats of music. The foot which leads the combination, as well as the direction (right, left, forward, back, in place, etc.), will be specified in the dance description.

For example, "right Cha Cha forward" instructs you to: on "1", step forward on your right foot; on "&", step forward on your left foot; on "2", step forward on your right foot.

A Cha Cha is much like a shuffle: both have three steps to a two beat, syncopated rhythm. However, in a Cha Cha the three steps are all the same size, whereas in a shuffle, the second step is shorter than the first and third. As there is no travelling in a "shuffle in place" or "Cha Cha in place", the "in place" versions of these combinations look identical.

Charleston Kick Instructs you to make four movements to four beats of music. The foot that begins (leads) the combination is specified. On beat one, the lead foot steps forward. On beat two, the following foot kicks forward. On beat three, the following foot steps back, and, on beat four, the lead foot touches back.

For example, "Right Charleston kick" instructs you: on "1", step your right foot forward; on "2", kick your left foot forward; on "3", step back on your left foot; on "4", touch your right toe back.

For a very advanced Charleston look, swivel your heels alternately out and in to a syncopated rhythm. (We have never seen this done on a Country and Western dance floor.)

Charleston Step Instructs you to make eight movements in four beats of music, beginning on a ½ beat. The pattern involves each foot swinging forward and back. The foot which leads (begins) the pattern will be specified. On the ½ beat before beat one, the lead foot is lifted slightly off the floor and is swung out to the side and forward. On "1", the lead foot touches forward. On "&", the lead foot is swung out to the side and back. On "2", the lead foot steps back. On "&", the following foot is swung out to the side and back. On "3", the following foot touches back. On "&", the following foot is swung out to the side and forward. On "4", the following foot steps forward. When done to music, these eight movements have the appearance of legs swinging smoothly from one position to the next.

For example, "right Charleston step" instructs you to swing your right foot out to the right side and forward, touch your right foot forward, swing your right foot out to the side and back, and step your right foot back. You then swing your left foot out to the left side and back, touch your left foot back, swing your left foot out to the left side and forward, and step forward on your left foot. These movements are done to a count of "and one and two and three and four."

In addition to foot movements, the Charleston step has arm movements that accompany it. Throughout the eight movements, the arms are essentially opposite one another (e.g. if the right arm is forward, the left arm is back). On the ½ beats, the arms are out to the sides. On the full beats, the arm opposite the lead foot is forward when the lead foot is forward and is back when the lead foot is back. As with the feet, when done to music, these eight movements have the appearance of arms swinging smoothly from one position to the next. For example, "right Charleston step" instructs you to swing your arms out to the sides, left arm forward, to the sides, left arm back, to the sides, left arm forward, to the sides, left arm back.
For a very advanced Charleston look, swivel your heels alternately out and in to a syncopated rhythm. (We have never seen this done on a Country and Western dance floor.)

Chug Instructs you to bend the knee of the leg specified and lift the leg slightly from the floor. This move is very much like a "hitch". The difference is one of degree. While in a hitch the thigh is nearly parallel to the floor, a chug is a much smaller move. In a chug, the foot is lifted only a few inches from the floor.

For example, "chug **left** leg" instructs you to bend your left knee as you lift your left foot slightly off the floor.

Clap Instructs you to clap your hands together, once, on the designated musical beat.

Coaster Step Instructs you to make three back and forward steps in two beats of music. The foot that leads the sequence will be identified in the dance description. On "1", the lead foot steps back. On "&", the following foot steps next to the lead foot. On "2", the lead foot steps forward. Because of the quick change of direction involved, the first two steps should be taken on the balls of the feet. This movement produces a look of the feet backing away from the body.

For example, "right coaster step" instructs you to: on "1", step back on the ball of your right foot, on "&", step the ball of your left foot next to your right, and on "2", step forward on your right foot.

D

Draw

Instructs you to slide the identified foot for a designated number of beats. The action is continuous, but slow. This move produces a look of the foot being pulled from one position to the next. At the conclusion of a draw, most or all of the body weight is supported by the drawn foot. A draw is similar in movement to a slide: they differ only in that a slide is completed in one beat of music. Note that a draw is different from a draw-up. In a draw, the sliding foot bears weight; in a draw-up, it does not.

For example, "for beats 1-3, Draw **left** foot next to **right** foot" specifies a three beat draw of the left foot. On beat one, you would begin to slide your left foot toward your right, and you would continue this motion through beat two. On beat three, the draw is completed with most or all of your weight transferred to your left foot.

Draw-up

Instructs you to slide the identified foot for a designated number of beats. The action is continuous, but slow. This move produces a look of the foot being pulled from one position to the next. When a draw-up is completed, the drawn foot is touching the floor but bears no weight. A draw-up is similar in movement to a slide-up: they differ only in that a slide-up is completed in one beat of music. Note that a draw is different from a draw-up. In a draw, the sliding foot bears weight; in a draw-up, it does not.

For example, "for beats 1-3, Draw-up **left** foot next to **right** foot" specifies a three beat draw-up of the left foot. On beat one, you would begin to slide your left foot toward your right, and you would continue this motion through beat two. On beat three, the draw is completed with the left foot touching the floor next to the right foot.

E

Electric Kick

Instructs you to make four movements in two beats of music. The foot which "kicks" will be identified in the dance description while the other foot "supports" the weight during the kick. On the half beat before "1", the support foot steps diagonally back. On "1", the heel of the kicking foot touches diagonally forward. On "&", the kicking foot steps home. On "2", the support foot touches or steps next to the kicking foot, depending on the action required next. (Electric Kicks are also known as "Romps".)

For example, "left electric kick" instructs you to: on "&" step diagonally back on your right foot; on "1", touch your left heel diagonally forward; on "&", step your left foot home, and on "2", touch your right foot next to your left foot.

Most dancers find the electric kick very difficult to do at first. As with all dance steps, it gets easier with practice. Practice it very slowly and mechanically at first. Start by practicing small movements, and then try separating your feet more and more as you gain familiarity with the moves. As you become proficient with this combination, your four movements will begin to look like two, and your kicking leg will appear to be "flying" to its heel touch.
Use caution when you first begin to practice this move.

F

Face Instructs you to change, temporarily, the orientation of your body. Face is used with foot directions to add body styling, but it does not change your reference point or wall. "Face" is different from "turn" in that "face" directs body orientation only for the beat(s) on which it appears, however, "turn" results in a permanent change of body orientation and a new reference point or wall.

Flare Instructs you to make a low kick, keeping the foot parallel to the floor. While a kick generally brings the foot about six inches off the floor, in a flare the foot is lifted only high enough to avoid touching the floor. The direction of the flare will be specified in the dance description.

Flare-Ball-Change Replaces the first move of a kick-ball-change with a flare forward. For example, "right flare-ball-change" on beats one and two instructs you to: on "1", flare your right foot forward (about one inch off the floor); on "&", step the ball of your right foot next to your left foot; on "2", step your left foot in place.

Flick Instructs you to kick the identified foot backward. In a flick, the toe points down.

H

Hand Movements Many dances include arm and hand movements as part of the pattern. Hand and arm movements may accompany foot movements or they may be the only activity choreographed for a sequence of beats.

Heel Click Instructs you to make two movements in one beat of music. On the half beat before one, swivel your right heel to the right and left heel to the left. On beat one, swivel the heels to the center until they meet, usually with a sound. To accomplish the heel click, be sure to keep your body weight over the balls of the feet. A heel click is a double-time heel split.

Heel Grind Instructs you to make two movements with the identified foot in one beat of music. On "1", with your foot turned in, step forward on your heel, the weight of your body placed on the heel. On "&", swivel your toe to the outside, keeping your weight on the heel.

For example, "right heel grind" instructs you to, on beat one, step forward on your right heel with foot turned in, and on "and", swivel your right toe from diagonally left to diagonally right.

Heel Split Instructs you to move your heels apart and then bring them back together in two beats of music. A heel split will begin from a position in which your feet are together and your weight is supported by both feet. On beat one, move your heels apart. To execute this move, have your weight on the balls of your feet and move your right heel to the right and your left heel to the left. On beat two, move your heels back together. (Heel splits are also called: "butterfies", "buttermilks", "pigeon toes", and "scissors".)

Heel Strut Instructs you to execute two moves in two beats of music. The foot involved in the strut will be specified in the dance description. On beat one, the heel of the specified foot is touched forward with the toe pointing up. On beat two, the toe of the specified foot is lowered as weight is transferred to that foot. Unlike toe struts, heel struts are always done moving forward.

For example, "left heel strut" instructs you, on "1", to touch your left heel forward, and on "2", to lower your left toe to the floor and step down.

Heel Twist Instructs you to make two movements in two beats of music. The foot which moves will be identified in the dance description. On beat one, the heel touches forward with foot turned in. On beat two, the toe swivels so that it moves from pointing inside to pointing forward and weight is placed on the foot (i.e. the foot steps down). Note: a heel twist is like a heel strut except that on beat one in a heel twist, the toes point up and inward, but in a heel strut the toes point up.

For example, "right heel twist" instructs you on "1", to touch your right heel forward with foot turned in, and on "2", keeping your heel touched to the floor, to swivel your right foot (so the toe points forward) and step down on your right foot.

Hip Roll Instructs you to move your hips around in a specified number of beats. The direction (clockwise or counter-clockwise), extent of rotation (half-circle or full circle) and the starting position of the hips (e.g. left diagonal back) will be specified in the dance description. The hip roll is a continuous movement over the specified beats of music. The hips begin a hip roll by moving out from under the body in the direction specified and remain out from under the body until they reach the roll's end position. As with a hip bump, hip rolls are generally easier to execute if the weight is supported by both feet and the knees are bent slightly. Unlike the hip bump, which is completed in a single beat of music, the hip roll will take several beats of music to complete.

For example, "beats 1-4 Full hip roll, counter-clockwise (begin left hip diagonally back)" instructs you to move your hips to the left diagonal back position (if they are not already there), push them to the right, then diagonally forward, and next, keeping the hips pushed out, circle them left and back until they reach their starting position.

Hitch Instructs you to bend your knee and raise your leg. During a hitch, the thigh of the hitching leg should be almost parallel to the floor. The feet should be parallel to each other.

Hold This one is easy. "Hold" instructs you to maintain your position, or do nothing for the designated beats of music.
For example, "hold" means do nothing.

Home Describes a position in which your feet are directly under your body and are parallel to one another. For example, when you are instructed to move your right foot "home", you are to return it to a comfortable standing position under your right hip. ("Home" is sometimes used to refer to your starting position on the dance floor, but that definition will not be used in this book.)

Hook Instructs you to bend your knee, raise your leg, and cross it in front of or behind the weighted leg. The leg to be hooked, and whether it crosses in front of or behind the weighted leg will be specified in the step description. The hooked leg crosses the weighted leg slightly below knee level. The foot of the hooked leg should be turned out. This movement is done in one beat of music. On occasion, a step description will instruct you to hook your leg to the side. In a hook to the side, the hooked leg will angle out to the side and the toe will point down.

For example, "hook **right** leg across **left** leg" instructs you to bend the knee of your right leg, lifting it off the floor, and to cross your right leg in front of your left leg. Your right foot should be turned out.

J

Jazz Box Instructs you to make three steps, in a specified order, to three beats of music. A jazz box will be described as either right or left, based on the foot that makes the crossing move and leads the jazz box. On beat one, the leading foot steps across the following foot. On beat two, the following foot steps back. On beat three, the leading foot steps to the side (parallel to and shoulder width away from the following foot). Note that you will touch three corners of an imaginary square (or box) as you make these three steps. (Jazz boxes are also called "jazz squares".)

As with vines, a fourth, "finishing move" for the foot that is free to move after the jazz box is often specified (and, actually, may complete the box). In some dances, rather than having a "finishing move", the jazz box is preceded by a step (to make up 4 steps). Some jazz box instructions may include turns (giving a funny look to the imaginary box). That is, you will see directions like "right jazz box with left step" or "right step with left jazz box" or "right jazz box with 1/4 turn right".

For example, "right jazz box with left step" instructs you to: step your right foot across your left foot, step your left foot back, step your right foot to the right side, and step your left foot next to your right foot, to a rhythm of 1, 2, 3, 4.

Jump Instructs you to jump in the specified direction, lifting and landing on both feet. Jumps are done to one beat of music.

Jump-Cross-Turn Instructs you to make two jumps and one turn in three beats of music. The direction of the turn will be specified in the dance description. On beat one, the dancer jumps, landing with both feet about shoulder width apart. On beat two, the dancer jumps again, landing with the legs crossed. The leg which is named by the direction of the turn must be crossed behind the other leg. On beat three, the dancer pivots 1/2 turn in the direction specified, "uncrossing" the legs. As with vines and many other three step combinations, a fourth, finishing move is often specified when a jump-cross-turn is used in 4/4 time music.

For example, "jump-cross-turn to the left" instructs you to: on "1", jump and land with feet apart; on "2", jump and land with left leg crossed behind right leg; on "3", pivot 1/2 turn to the left on the balls of both feet.

Some dancers find jump-cross-turns too jarring, especially when several are done in rapid succession. Because of this, an alternative to the jump-cross-turn has been developed. It proceeds as follows: on "1", touch, to the side, the toe of the foot opposite the direction of the turn; on "2", step the foot opposite the direction of the turn across the other foot (leaving weight on both feet); on "3", pivot 1/2 turn in the direction specified (as in the jump-cross-turn).

For example, (replacing a jump-cross-turn to the left): on beat one, touch your right toe to the right side; on beat two, step your right foot across your left foot; on beat three, pivot 1/2 turn to the left on the balls of both feet.

K

Kick Instructs you to kick the specified foot about half-way between the floor and knee-height. Kicks are most often done forward, but the direction of the kick will be specified in the step instruction. In country dancing, kicks are done with the toes pointing up, as if to shake something off the boot.

Kick-Ball-Change Instructs you to make three steps, in a specified order, to two beats of music. The foot that begins or leads the kick-ball-change will be specified in the dance description. On the first beat of a kick-ball-change, the leading foot is kicked forward (about six inches off the floor). On the half beat, the ball of the leading foot steps next to the following foot. On the second beat, the following foot steps in place. The dancer should note that this third movement is subtle. The following foot has not moved: it has simply stepped in place. An alternative way to think of this third movement is as a transfer of body weight from the leading foot to the following foot.

For example, "right kick-ball-change" instructs you to kick your right foot forward, step the ball of your right foot next to your left, and step your left foot in place, to a count of "one-and-two".

L

Latin- "Latin-" is used as a prefix with a variety of steps and instructs you to sway your hips in the direction of the moving foot. This sway is a fluid movement of the hips from one location to the next, and is unlike the bump, which is sharp and pronounced.

For example, "Latin-step **left** foot to left side" instructs you to step to the left, swaying your left hip to the left as you take the step.

Lindy Instructs you to make a sideways shuffle and two rocks in four beats of music. The direction of movement will be specified in the dance description.

For example, "right Lindy" instructs you to: on "1&2", do a right shuffle to the right side; on "3", rock-step your left foot behind your right foot, as you face diagonally left; on "4", rock forward on your right foot, still facing diagonally left.

This combination produces a look of pulling away from a starting point and being "sprung" back to it. The shuffle and the first rock move smoothly in one direction. On the last rock, you will look as though you are being tugged back toward your starting point.

Lock Indicates a foot position in which one leg is crossed tightly over the other.

For example, "Slide **left** foot back to lock across **right** foot" indicates that at the end of the slide, the left leg should be crossed over the right leg.

Lunge Instructs you to take a long step in the indicated direction, bending the knee of the stepping leg. When the step is forward, the move is like a fencing lunge.

M

Military Turn Instructs you to make a 180 degree (½) turn in two beats of music. The direction of the turn (right or left) will always be specified. On beat one, the foot opposite the direction of the turn steps forward. On beat two, the body makes a ½ turn in the direction specified, pivoting on the balls of both feet. A "military turn" includes only one instruction for a change of foot location – at the close of a military turn the dancer will be standing with one foot in front of the other.

For example, "military turn to the left" instructs you to, on beat one, step forward on your right foot and, on beat two, pivot ½ turn left on the balls of both feet. At the close of a "military turn to the left" the dancer will be standing with feet separated and with the right foot behind the left.

Monterey Turn Instructs you to make a ½ turn in four beats of music. The direction of the turn will be specified in the dance description. On "1", touch the lead foot (the foot in the direction of the turn) to the side. On "2", on the ball of the following foot, pivot ½ turn in the direction specified. Step the lead foot next to the following foot as the turn is completed. On "3", touch the toe of the following foot to the side. On "4", step the following foot next to the lead foot.

For example, "Monterey turn to the right" instructs you to: on beat one, touch your right toe to the side; on beat two, pivot ½ turn to the right on your left foot, stepping your right foot next to your left as you complete this turn; on beat three, touch your left toe to the left side; on beat four, step your left foot next to your right.

P

Paddle Turn Instructs you to make a turn while you alternate weight from your "anchor" foot (the foot in the direction of the turn) to your "paddle" foot. In a paddle turn you will make a series of small turns in order to complete a ¼, ½, ¾ or full turn. Each small turn will begin by stepping the "anchor" foot in place, but toward the direction of the turn.

The "paddling" foot will next step to a position parallel to the anchor foot and about shoulder width apart. The paddle turn has the look of a boat going around in a circle as it is paddled with one oar. The number of beats it will take to execute the turn, the total amount of the turn, and the direction of the paddle turn will be specified in the dance description.

For example, "beats 1-4 ¼ Paddle turn to the left" instructs you to: on beat one, step your left foot in place and turned out (i.e. pointed diagonally left); on beat two, step your right foot parallel to your left foot about shoulder width apart (completing a ⅛ turn to the left); on beat three, step your left foot in place and turned out; and on beat four, step your right foot parallel to your left about shoulder width apart (completing another ⅛ turn to the left).

Parallel Indicates that one foot is held in essentially the same direction as the other foot. "Parallel" for you should be your comfortable standing position.

Pivot Instructs you to turn. The amount of the turn will be specified (¼ or 90 degrees, ½ or 180 degrees, etc.), as will the direction of the turn (right or left). Pivots are usually done on the ball of the designated foot (or feet), however, on occasion a pivot is done on the heel of one foot and the ball of the other. Pivots are easier if you "prepare" your pivoting foot by slightly pointing it in the direction of the turn before you step down to pivot.

For example, "pivot on left foot ¼ turn left" instructs you to turn 90 degrees left while your weight is supported by your left foot. You would begin this move by pointing your left foot diagonally left. The move is completed by pivoting the rest of the ¼ turn on the ball of your left foot.

Place Instructs you to execute a foot action without changing the foot's location. In these cases you will be told to do the action "in place". For example, if you are told to "step **right** foot in place", you are to put weight on your right foot, wherever it was after your preceding move.

Polka Instructs you to make a shuffle and one other movement in two and a half beats of music. The direction of the polka (forward, backward, or to the side) and the foot that begins, or leads, the polka will be specified in the dance description. The three shuffle steps take place on beats one and two. The fourth step, which takes place on the next half-beat after beat two, may be a kick, turn, or hop and will be specified in the dance description. The steps are done to a rhythm of "one-and-two-and".

For example, "right polka forward with ½ turn left" instructs you to: on "1", step forward on your right foot; on "&", step the ball of your left foot next to heel of your right foot; on "2", step forward on your right foot; and on "&", pivot ½ turn left on the ball of your right foot.

R

Rock Instructs you to move your body in the direction specified, over the foot that is in that location. The instruction, "rock", refers to movement of the body, and not the feet. If the dancer needs to move the foot in order to execute the body movement, the term "rock-step" is used. A rock is easier to execute if the knees are bent slightly.

For example, "rock forward on **right** foot" instructs you to move, or rock, your body forward, over your right foot.

Rock-step Instructs you to step in the direction specified, but unlike a simple "step", it requires you to lean your body in the direction of the step. If the dancer does not need to move the foot in order to execute the body movement, the term "rock" is used. A rock-step is easier to execute if the knees are bent slightly.

For example, "rock-step **left** foot back" instructs you to step back on your left foot and lean your body slightly back, over your left foot, as you take this step.

Rondé Instructs you to move the designated foot in an arc. The amount of movement (¼ or ½ circle), the beginning position, and the beats in which the movement must be completed, will be specified in the dance description. The moving foot is either on the floor, or raised slightly above it. The rondé is generally easier to execute if the knee of the leg supporting your weight is bent slightly. (Rondé is also known as rond de jambe.)

For example, "right ¼ rondé (begin forward)" instructs you to touch your right toe forward and, leaving your leg extended, draw a quarter circle with your right toe, ending at the right side position.

S

Sailor step Instructs you to make three foot movements in two beats of music. The foot to lead (begin) the pattern, and whether it steps across or behind, will be specified. On beat one, the lead foot steps across or behind the following foot. On the ½ beat, the following foot steps to the side. On beat two, the lead foot steps to the side. When a sailor step is completed, the feet are about shoulder width apart. In a sailor step, the body leans slightly in the direction of the foot to move first.

For example, "right sailor step (begin behind)" instructs you to step your right foot behind your left, step your left foot to the left side, and step your right foot to the right side. These movements are done to a count of "one and two". Throughout a right sailor step, you would lean slightly to the right.

Scoot Instructs you to take a small jump or hop slightly forward on the identified foot. This movement is subtle: you neither move very far nor come high off the floor.

Scuff Instructs you to bring your heel in contact with the floor while you move your foot forward. This will make a noise and that is important in Country and Western dancing. Scuff sounds are often chosen to accentuate the rhythmic beats in the music to which the dance is done. The scuff involves no weight transfer.

For example, "scuff left foot" instructs you to push or scrape your left heel against the floor. In "scuff left foot" the right foot supports your weight during and after the scuff.

Shimmy Describes an upper body movement in which the shoulders alternately are moved forward and backward in syncopated rhythm (i.e. on beats and half-beats).

For example, "for beats 1-4, Shimmy shoulders" tells you to: on "1", move your right shoulder forward (left goes back), on "&" move your left shoulder forward, on "2", move your right shoulder forward, on "&" move left shoulder forward, and so on.

Dance descriptions may call for shimmies with or without foot movements. Some individuals inadvertently do hip wiggles instead of shimmies, and these hip movements may interfere with foot movements. Thus, alternatives to shimmies, which do not interfere with foot movements, may be offered as "variations".

Shuffle Instructs you to make three steps, in a specified order, to two beats of music. The direction of the shuffle (forward, backward, or to the side) and the foot that begins, or leads, the shuffle, will be specified in the dance description. On the first beat of music in a shuffle, the leading foot steps in the direction specified. On the half beat, the ball of the following foot steps next to the heel of the leading foot. On the second beat of music, the leading foot again steps in the specified direction. In a shuffle, feet are gently dragged or barely lifted from position to position.

For example, "right shuffle forward" instructs you to step forward on your right foot, step the ball of your left foot next to heel of your right foot, and step forward on your right foot, to a rhythm of "one-and-two".

A shuffle is different from a Cha Cha. Like a shuffle, the Cha Cha includes three steps to two beats of music. In a shuffle, however, the second step does not move beyond the lead foot, while in a Cha Cha, the three steps are equally long.

Slap Instructs you to slap your foot (or other identified body part). The instruction will identify the slapping hand and the body part. The left hand always slaps the left side of the designated parts and the right hand slaps the right side.

Slide Instructs you to move the designated foot while keeping it lightly in contact with the floor. This move produces a look of the foot being pulled from one position to the next. When a slide is completed, all or most of the weight is on the sliding foot. Note that a slide is different from a slide-up. In a slide, the sliding foot bears weight; in a slide-up, it does not.

For example, "slide **right** foot next to **left** foot" instructs you to move your right foot from its last position to a position next to your left foot, keeping your right foot lightly in contact with the floor. As you finish the move, put all or most of your weight on the right foot.

Slide-up Instructs you to move the designated foot while keeping it lightly in contact with the floor. This move produces a look of the foot being pulled from one position to the next. When a slide-up is completed, the sliding foot is touching the floor but bears no weight. Note that a slide is different from a slide-up. In a slide, the sliding foot bears weight; in a slide-up, it does not.

For example, "slide-up **right** foot next to **left** foot" instructs you to move your right foot from its last position to a position next to your left foot, while keeping your right foot lightly in contact with the floor.

Slow Instructs you to perform the designated step over two beats of music rather than one. For example, "slow touch **right** heel forward" instructs you to use two beats of music to touch your right heel to the floor. Initially, the slow move may feel clumsy and seem difficult to do. It may help to think about a slow heel touch as a chug on beat one and a heel touch on beat two.
Most steps are choreographed to match one beat of music. Although not used in this book, a step done to one beat of music is often called a "quick" step. It is in contrast to the name "quick" that steps done to two beats of music are called "slow". Steps done on half-beats of music are often called "syncopated".

Step Instructs you to position your foot at the identified location and to transfer all or most of your weight to that foot. The amount of weight transferred usually depends on the sequence of steps.

For example, "step **right** foot forward" instructs you to position your right foot ahead of your left (as though you were walking forward), with your weight supported on your right foot, leaving your left foot ready to move next.

Stomp Instructs you to bring the identified foot down with force, transferring weight to the stomping foot. This will make a noise and, as with scuffs, stomp sounds are often used to accentuate the beats of the music. A "stomp" differs from a "stomp-up" in that in a "stomp" the stomping foot bears weight, but in a "stomp-up" it does not.

For example, "stomp **right** foot next to **left** foot" instructs you to bring your right foot down with force next to your left. Your right foot supports all or most of your weight after the stomp.

Stomp-up Instructs you to bring the identified foot down with force, without a weight transfer to the stomping foot. This will make a noise and, as with scuffs, stomp sounds are often used to accentuate the beats of the music. A "stomp" differs from a "stomp-up" in that in a "stomp" the stomping foot bears weight, but in a "stomp-up" it does not.

For example, "stomp-up **right** foot next to **left** foot" instructs you to bring your right foot down with force next to your left. Your left foot supports your weight during and after the stomp.

Sugar Foot Instructs you to make a heel and toe touch of a designated foot to two beats of music. In the sugar foot, sometimes the heel touches first and sometimes the toe touches first; the order will be specified in the dance description. The heel and toe touches are both done next to the weighted foot. On the heel touches, the sugar foot is turned out. On the toe touches, the sugar foot is turned in.

For example, "Right toe-heel sugar foot" instructs you to, on "1", touch your right toe next to your left foot (right foot turned in), and on "2", touch your right heel next to your left foot (right foot turned out).

Swivel heels Instructs you to turn both heels in the direction specified (i.e. left, right or center). Movement is executed by supporting the weight on the balls of both feet and turning the heels approximately 45 degrees in the direction indicated. While your feet move in this step, your body continues to face forward. Note that a "swivel" is different from a "twist" in which your body would be allowed to move with your feet. Note also, "swivel heels" (in which your heels are turned) is different from "swivel toes" (in which your toes are turned).

For example, "swivel heels to left" instructs you to put your body weight over the balls of both feet and turn your heels to the left. Note that when you complete this move, your toes will be pointed to the right. "Swivel heels to center" instructs you to return your heels to their starting position under your body.

Swivel toes Instructs you to turn both toes in the direction specified (i.e. left, right or center). Movement is executed by supporting the weight on the heels of both feet and turning the toes approximately 45 degrees in the direction indicated. While your feet move in this step, your body continues to face forward. Note that a "swivel" is different from a "twist" in which your body would be allowed to move with your feet. Note, also, that toe swivels differ from heel swivels in which you move your heels while supporting your weight on your toes.

For example, "swivel toes to left" instructs you to put your body weight over the heels of both feet and turn your toes to the left. Note that when you complete this move, your toes will be pointed to the left. "Swivel toes to center" instructs you to return your toes to their starting position under your body.

Swivet Instructs you to swivel both feet, on the heel of one and ball of the other. Both feet turn approximately 45 degrees in the direction specified and then back to center in two beats of music. The direction of the swivet identifies the direction your toes will point on the first movement. The foot named in the direction of the swivet swivels its toe and the other foot swivels its heel. While swiveling, your weight will be on the heel of one foot and the ball of the other. At the completion of a swivet, both feet will be centered under your body and flat on the floor.

For example, "swivet to right" instructs you to: on "1", swivel your right toe to the right and your left heel to the left; on "2", swivel your right toe to center and your left heel to center.

Syncopated pattern Indicates a set of steps that deviate from the standard step pattern for a particular type of dance. For example, the standard step pattern for a waltz consists of three steps, either left-right-left or right-left-right. In a waltz, a set of steps like "step left, brush right, hitch right" (left-right-right) would represent a deviation from the standard and would be called "syncopated".

Syncopated rhythm Most dance steps are choreographed to match full beats of music. On occasion, steps are choreographed also for half-beats. Moving on half versus full beats makes a big difference in the overall look of a dance. In this book, when a dance requires a movement on a half beat, that half beat is labelled with the symbol "&" placed between full beats: "&" should be read as "and".

T

Three-Step Turn Instructs you to make one full turn in three steps to three beats of music. The turn will be labelled right or left, indicating the direction of the turn and the foot that leads the combination. On "1", step your lead foot to the side and pivot ½ turn in the indicated direction. On "2", step your following foot to the side and pivot another ½ turn in the indicated direction. On "3", step your lead foot to the side.

For example, a "three-step turn to left" means: on beat one, step your left foot to your left side and pivot ½ turn left; on beat "2", step your right foot to your right side and pivot ½ turn to the left; on beat"3", step your left foot to your left.

Although we do not use this label, three-step turns are sometimes called "rolling vines". Three-step turns are often done as variations in place of vines or step-slide-step patterns. When three-step turns are used in 4/4 time music, a fourth finishing move is often specified with the turn.

Toe Fan Instructs you to make two swivel movements of the identified foot in two beats of music. On "1", the toe swivels away from the stationary foot. On "2", the toe swivels to center.
For example, "right toe fan" instructs you, on beat one, to swivel your right toe to the right and, on beat two, to swivel your right toe to center.

Toe Strut Instructs you to execute two movements of one foot in two beats of music. The strutting foot, and the direction of the strut (i.e. forward or backward) will be specified in the dance description. On beat one, the toe is touched in the direction of travel. On beat two, the heel is lowered and weight is transferred to that foot.

For example, "left toe strut forward" instructs you: on "1", to touch your left toe forward and on "2", lower your left heel to the floor and step down on your left foot.

Touch Instructs you to position your foot at the identified location without a weight transfer. Except when a direction is given to touch with a heel, touches are typically done with the toe of the boot.

For example, "touch **right** foot next to **left** foot" instructs you to bring your right foot next to your left and lightly touch the floor, leaving your right foot ready to move next.

Touch-Ball-Change Replaces the first move of a kick-ball-change with a toe touch forward.

For example, "right touch-ball-change" for beats 1 and 2 instructs you to: on "1", touch your right toe forward; on "&", step the ball of your right foot next to your left foot; on "2", step your left foot in place.

Travelling Sugar Foot Specifies either a right or left sideways movement in two beats of music. In a travelling sugar foot, the leg opposite the direction to be travelled supports the weight alternately on heel and toe, while the other leg does a heel-toe sugar foot. On beat one, the weighted foot swivels its toe in the direction of travel. At the same time, the other heel touches, also with toe pointed in the direction of travel, next to the weighted foot. On beat two, the weighted foot swivels its heel in the direction of travel. At the same time, the other toe is touched, also with heel pointed in the direction of travel, next to the weighted foot. Note, on each beat both feet will be pointed in the same direction. This combination produces a look of gliding across the floor. Most dancers find this move to be very awkward at first. It gets much easier with practice.

For example, "travelling sugar foot to the right" instructs you, on beat one, to swivel your left toe to the right and touch your right heel next to your left foot, so that both toes will be pointed diagonally right. On beat two, swivel your left heel to the right and touch your right toe next to your left foot so that both toes point diagonally left.

Turn Indicates that the orientation of your body (direction or wall that you face) will change. There are different kinds of turns (pivot, military turn, etc.). Instructions to turn will specify a direction and amount of turn. Sometimes dancers become confused with the direction specified for a turn. To turn left means to turn counterclockwise. One way to ensure that you are turning in the prescribed direction is to think of your shoulders. In a turn to the left, you will turn toward your left shoulder. Your left shoulder will move backwards, while your right shoulder moves forward. Similarly, in a turn to the right, you will turn toward your right shoulder. Your right shoulder will move backwards, while your left shoulder moves forward. The amount of turn may be given as fractions of a full circle (1/8, 1/4, 1/2, etc.) or in degrees (90 degrees, 180 degrees, etc.)

Turned In Indicates that the toe of one foot points diagonally toward the other foot. When the right foot is "turned in" its toe points diagonally left. When the left foot is "turned in" its toe points diagonally right.

Turned Out Indicates that the toe of one foot points diagonally away from the other. When the right foot is "turned out" its toe points diagonally right. When the left foot is "turned out" its toe points diagonally left.

Twist Instructs you to turn your body without lifting your feet from the floor. The direction of the twist (diagonally right or diagonally left) will be specified. Often, after a series of twists, "twist center" will instruct you to return your body to a forward facing position. Twists are easier to execute if the knees are bent slightly and the weight is over the balls of the feet, not the heels.

For example, "twist left" instructs you to turn your body diagonally left by supporting your weight on the balls of your feet and moving your heels to the right.

V

Vine Instructs you to make a three step sideways movement to three beats of music. A vine will be described as either a right vine or left vine, indicating the direction of movement and the foot that moves first. On the first beat, the designated foot will move to the side. On the second beat, the other foot is crossed behind the first before it steps down. On the third beat, the foot that was first to move, moves again to the side.

For example, "right vine" instructs you to: step your right foot to the right, step your left foot behind your right, and then step your right foot to the right.

When vines are used in 4/4 time music, a fourth, "finishing move" for the foot that is free to move after the vine is often specified with the vine. For example, you will see directions like "right vine with left scuff" or "left vine with right touch".

If the movement of a vine is not directly to the side, the direction of movement will be specified (for example, left vine diagonally back). Vines are also referred to as "grapevines". Other dance descriptions may use "vine" or "grapevine" to describe combinations other than the one described above. That is, combinations that begin with a step other than the side step or combinations that include more than one cross step are called vines. To avoid confusion, we use other labels to refer to these less common vines (see, for example, "weave").

W

Weave Instructs you to make a series of movements in which steps across and behind alternate with steps to the side. The first step in a weave will always be across or behind. The number of beats involved in the weave will be specified in the dance description and each step will be done to one beat of music. The direction of the weave (examples, "to left" or "diagonally right") and whether the first move is across or behind will be specified in the dance description.
Note: because weaves begin with the first foot to move stepping across or behind, the first foot to move is the foot opposite the direction of the weave.

For example, "beats 1- 4 Weave to right (begin across)" tells you to: on "1", step your left foot across your right, on "2", step your right foot to the right side, on "3", step your left foot behind your right, and on "4", again step your right foot to the right side.

Doing a weave may feel very much like doing a vine. In fact, a weave is a special type of vine. It is different from the vines you have danced so far in that it begins with a crossing step, and the crossing steps are alternately in front of and behind the weighted foot.

Weighted leg Refers to the leg supporting the weight of the body.

Wiggle Describes a body movement in which the hips and the shoulders move in opposition to one another. They are moved forward and backward in syncopated rhythm (i.e. on beats and half-beats). For example, on "1", the right shoulder moves forward and the right hip moves back; on "and", the right shoulder moves back and the right hip moves forward; on "two", the right shoulder moves forward and the right hip moves back. Wiggles may accompany steps and other body movements (for example, as you lower your body to a squat or raise your body to a standing position). The initial direction of hip and shoulder movements is not specified: do what is most comfortable for you.

More Books from . . .

We publish a wide range of books (currently over 200!), many for outdoor pursuits including walking, cycling, football & golf. We also publish excellent general interest books – and here is a selection:

Mildred Smith's Favourite Family Recipes

Published in association with **GRANADA TELEVISION**, this is the second cookery book from Mildred Smith – the much-loved traditional cookery star of Granada TV's "The Main Ingredient". In this, you'll find many famous traditional recipes for everything from a simple sauce through satisfying main courses to delicious deserts; including such tempting treats as sticky toffee pudding, banoffee pie and other sweets too nice to mention. *£6.95*

Caravan and Holiday Cookery

You don't like take-away food, but you don't want to spend your entire holiday slaving over a hot stove. So how can you preserve your sanity and keep the family happy? Here's the answer – simple cookery using some ready-made items plus readily available fresh food. Over 100 tempting meals, none of which need more than two rings and a grill. Lemon minted cod in 10 minutes – apple and coriander chicken in half an hour – oat crunch in no time at all. Why queue in a take-away? *£4.95*

Exercises That Work For You: Non-strenuous fitness basics for body, mind and spirit

For many years, Elizabeth Graham Smith has run exercise and Tai Chi classes. In this book, she passes on her exercise programme for whole body and mind fitness. Her holistic message goes right through the book: fitness is a composite matter: tense muscles accompany tense minds and spirits; allow mind and spirit more freedom and some psychological hang-ups can vanish! *£6.95*